MANIFOLD DESTINY

Manifold

- - - - - - - - - - - - - -

Destiny

- - - - - - - - - - - - - -

THE ONE! THE ONLY! GUIDE TO COOKING ON YOUR CAR ENGINE!

REVISED AND UPDATED

Chris Maynard and Bill Scheller

VILLARD NEW YORK

All rights reserved under International and
Pan-American Copyright Conventions.
Published in the United States by Villard Books,
a division of Random House, Inc., New York,
and simultaneously in Canada by Random House
of Canada Limited, Toronto.

Villard Books is a registered trademark of Random House, Inc.

This is a revised edition of *Manifold Destiny,* which was published in 1989 by
Villard Books, a division of Random House, Inc.

LIBRARY OF CONGRESS CATALOGING-IN-PUBLICATION DATA
Maynard, Chris
Manifold destiny: the one! the only! guide to cooking on your car engine/by
Chris Maynard and Bill Scheller.
p. cm.
ISBN 0-375-75140-8
1. Cookery.   2. Automobiles—Motors.   I. Scheller, Bill.   II. Title.
TX652.M335   1989
641.5'8—dc20   89-40194

All interior photographs by Chris Maynard
Book design by Oksana Kushnir

Random House website address: www.randomhouse.com
Printed in the United States of America on acid-free paper

2   4   6   8   9   7   5   3

Revised Edition

FOR PLUGGY AND MOLLY

CONTENTS

1. IN WHICH WE GET STARTED, AND ASK
   THE QUESTION "WHY BOTHER?"   3

2. BEGINNER'S LUCK—AND SKILLS   13

3. CAR-ENGINE RECIPES: FOUR AMERICAN
   REGIONAL CUISINES   57

4. CAR-ENGINE RECIPES: INTERNATIONAL
   CAR CUISINE   127

   APPENDIX: RECIPE LIST BY REGION   148

MANIFOLD DESTINY

IN WHICH WE GET STARTED, AND ASK THE QUESTION "WHY BOTHER?"

Traffic has smelled a lot better over the past nine years.

That's how long it's been since the original edition of *Manifold Destiny* appeared. Nine years! Seems like it went by in a flash, unless you're one of the people who went overboard and tried to do a standing rib roast or a whole turkey, in which case you probably just now stopped driving. We hope your car radio works—otherwise, there's a lot we have to tell you. George Bush became president and threw up on the prime minister of Japan. We fought a war in the Mideast, which is why you had enough gas to finish the turkey. Bill Clinton became president but hasn't thrown up on anyone yet. That white Ford Bronco you passed in L.A. a few years back, the one going real slow . . . oh, never mind. Lots of stuff happened—but most important of all, *Manifold Destiny* has become a cult classic.

We could go on and on about how secondhand-book sellers can't keep the original *Manifold Destiny* in stock.

About how we became so popular in Germany—either in spite of or because of the fact that there's no German-language edition of the book—that we were flown over to appear on a live variety show in Dortmund (fortunately, Bush didn't ruin our reception by throwing up on Helmut Kohl). About how our lives have changed immeasurably, allowing us to hang out in Gstaad and St. Barts with glamorous celebrities. But in case you're new to all this, let's start instead by telling you that, to this day, neither of us can leave Montreal without stopping first at Schwartz's, on Boulevard St.-Laurent.

Schwartz's is a little storefront deli that cures and smokes its own beef briskets, which it heaps high in the front window partly for display and partly so the countermen can quickly spear and slice them. "Smoked meat" is what Montreal prosaically calls this apotheosis of pastrami, and Schwartz's makes the best. You can eat it in the store. You can take it out and eat it at home. Or you may have to eat it on the sidewalk half a block away when the aroma coming through the butcher paper drives you nuts. What we had in mind, one summer's day in 1984, was to pack some in the car for a rest-stop picnic on our way back to Boston.

We were barely out of the city when we started to talk about what a shame it was that our pound of Schwartz's wouldn't be so alluringly hot when we pulled over for lunch. When you order this stuff the way Montreal insiders do—"easy on the lean"—room temperature just doesn't do it justice.

It was then that the idea hit. One of us remembered those stories we used to hear thirty years ago, about lonely truckers cooking hot dogs and beans on their engines. Why not Schwartz's smoked meat? It wouldn't even be cooking it—Schwartz had already done that—

but just borrowing a little heat from the engine to warm it up. So we decided what the hell; if it worked for Teamsters, why not us?

We pulled off the interstate in Burlington, Vermont, bought a roll of aluminum foil, and triple-wrapped the sliced brisket. Opening the hood, we spied a nice little spot under the air filter of the '84 VW Rabbit, which seemed the perfect place to tuck in the package, and off we went. An hour later, we arrived at a standard-issue Vermont highway rest stop, the kind that looks like they wash the trees, and *voilà!*—in minutes, we were putting away hot smoked-meat sandwiches that actually had steam rising off them. Best of all, we nearly made two women at the next picnic table choke on their sprouts when they saw that instead of a busted fan belt, we had actually just dragged our lunch from the Rabbit's greasy maw.

Necessity, to rewrite the old chestnut, is the mother of necessary inventions—like ways to heat smoked meat when you don't have a steam table handy. But since inspired foolishness is the *real* hallmark of civilization, it wasn't long before we were inventing necessities. For instance, a dire need to roast a pork tenderloin on I-95 between Philadelphia and Providence. Car engines, we discovered, are good for a lot more than simply heating things up.

Soon we were calling each other (not on car phones, thank God) with news of our latest accomplishments:

"I poached a fillet of sole."

"I roasted a stuffed eggplant."

"I figured out how to do game hens."

"I made baked apples."

Before long, those rest-stop stares of disbelief had been replaced by reactions infinitely more delightful to savor—like that of the toll collector who swore he smelled chicken and tarragon, but couldn't figure out where the hell it was coming from.

What we didn't realize, during those early years of random experimentation, was that our burgeoning skills as car-engine cooks were going to serve us splendidly as we competed in one of the most grueling sporting events on the planet: the Cannonball One Lap of America Rally. The One Lap was an eight-thousand-mile-plus highway marathon, seven days of nonstop driving in which participants had to adhere to strict rules while reeking of spilled coffee and unchanged underwear. It might have been the most exhausting and disorienting event anyone ever paid money to enter, but it made you feel like a kid with nothing to do except ride his bike in the park for a week—with no grown-ups around. It was so much fun, in fact, they don't run it anymore.

It was damned difficult to stick to the rally routes and get anything decent to eat. Most people who run the One Lap follow a regimen of truck-stop breakfasts (not necessarily eaten at breakfast time) and assorted pack-along calories drawn from the canned and bottled food groups. Our wonderful epiphany, shared by none of the fifty-seven other teams in the 1988 event, was that if we cooked on the big V-8 under the hood of our sponsor's stretched Lincoln Town Car, we could eat like epicures without screwing up our time and distance factors.

Here's what we did. Two days before the rally started in Detroit, we worked out a menu and did our shopping. Then we commandeered the kitchen of our friend Marty Kohn, a feature writer for the *Detroit Free Press*, and put together enough uncooked entrées to last us at least all the way to our midway layover in Los Angeles. Boneless chicken breasts with prosciutto and provolone, fillet of flounder, a whole pork tenderloin, a ham steak (a reversion to our simple heat-through days)—everything was seasoned, stuffed, and splashed according to our own recipes, sealed up tightly in three layers of aluminum foil, and promptly frozen. We felt like we were turning Marty's kitchen into a tiny suburban version of those factories where they make airplane food, with one big difference—our stuff was good.

The next day, we transferred our frosty little aluminum packages to the kitchen freezer at the Westin Hotel in the Renaissance Center (try pulling a request like *that* on the next concierge you meet) and had them brought up with our coffee and croissants on the morning of the rally. The food went into a cooler, the cooler went into our Lincoln, and off we went. Every afternoon between Detroit and the West Coast, we'd haul out another dinner, throw it on the engine, and cook it as we lopped a few hundred more miles off the route. Let our competitors use the drive-throughs at McDonald's. We ate well, very well indeed.

We would have done the same thing in L.A. for the return trip, but we didn't have the time. Anyway, it occurred to us somewhere around Albuquerque that we *couldn't* have done it, since none of the people we know in L.A. have freezers. Everyone there eats out all the time, subsisting entirely on selections from the foccacia, baby field greens, and roasted-garlic food groups.

By the time the rally ended, we'd gained more fame for our means of sustenance than for our position in the final standings: Everybody, it seemed, had something to say about car-engine cooking. Half the comments were expressions of pure disbelief (and this book is an attempt to convert the disbelievers), while the rest amounted to variations on "Truck drivers have been doing that for years."

Please. All the truck drivers we've ever heard of who cook on their diesels are still punching vent holes in cans of Dinty Moore stew.

This is not to say we refuse to acknowledge the pioneers. We are by no means the first people to cook food on car engines. The idea dates back so far, in fact, that it predates cars altogether.

The Huns of the fourth and fifth centuries lived on horseback, and subsisted to a great extent on meat. When a Hun wanted to enjoy a hunk of unsmoked brisket—say, when he was tearing around in the One Lap of the Western Roman Empire (with points for pillage)—he would take the meat and put it under his saddle cloth, and the friction between Hun and horse would have a tenderizing and warming effect. (We think they used saddle cloths. If not, well, just don't think about it.) Since this

was a situation in which a "cooking" effect was achieved by the application of excess heat generated by the means of propulsion, it is clearly part of the line of descent that leads to hot lunch buckets in the cab of a steam locomotive, and to stuffed chicken breasts à la Lincoln Town Car. We can't say for sure, but it may also have been the origin of steak tartare. In any event, it *did* give rise to the expression, "I'm home, Hun, what's for dinner?"

But let's get back to that important qualification—*excess heat generated by the means of propulsion*. This disqualifies a lot of other attempts at mobile cookery, or at least relegates them to a different branch of evolution. We read recently, for instance, that the big, handsomely outfitted carriage Napoleon Bonaparte used during his military campaigns was equipped with an oil lantern mounted above and behind the rear seat that could be used for cooking as well as lighting. But whether or not the little corporal used his lantern to heat up leftover veal Marengo, the fact is that lanterns don't make carriages go.

What Napoleon was really onto here was the ancestor of the dashboard microwave. When we first wrote *Manifold Destiny,* these were being touted as the next big thing for people who were so ludicrously busy they didn't even have time to zap fake pastry at home. Back then, we predicted that traffic accidents of the near future would involve some boob peeling a memo off his onboard fax machine and therefore not seeing the lady in the next lane taking a Pop-Tart out of her microwave. Little did we know that cockpit micros would never make it big because the real badge of honor among the upwardly mobile in the nineties would be *not to eat at all* but simply to carry little bottles of spring water with open-shut nipples on them. (It's a wonder carmakers don't rename their ubiquitous cup holders "rehydration modules," or some damned thing.) No, the really scary highway threat as we approach millennium's end is the onboard computer, which a certain Seattle nabob (who drives a Lexus, of all things, as if there were no Duesenbergs left on this Earth) is pushing as a means of checking your stocks and surfing the Net while you change lanes. And people thought eating and driving at the same time was dangerous!

Car-engine cooking is ridiculously safe by comparison. Since you can't check to see if your dinner is done without getting out of the vehicle and looking under the hood, it's no more dangerous than pulling over to change a tire—a lot less dangerous, in fact, since you don't get to pick the location for a flat tire.

But cooking on your engine is more than just a way to amuse yourself on the road without resorting to the high-tech totems of obsessive-compulsive "I'm-so-busy" behavior. Ultimately, it's all about getting some decent chow. Unless you're carrying with you the collected works of Calvin Trillin or Jane and Michael Stern and have the time to detour to all the wonderful diners and rib joints they have chronicled, a long car trip is likely to bring you up short in the eats department.

It's not like the good old days were any better. We recently came across Henry Miller's *The Air-Conditioned Nightmare,* based on a six-month cross-country trip he took in a '32 Buick back in 1941. Miller finished the trip in Los Angeles, not only dyspeptic over the philistines and materialists he claimed to have encountered all over the republic, but with his innards devastated from eating in one greasy spoon after another. Poor devil—that '32 Buick probably had a lovely flathead six, as choice a cooking device as any six-burner restaurant range. If only he'd known. And being Henry Miller, he'd probably have felt better about America if only he'd known that in little more than a decade, the philistines and materialists at Rambler were going to produce a car with a backseat that folded into a bed.

But we digress. The point is that you can make better meals for yourself, on your engine, than the vast majority of the roadside stands can make for you. Not to mention that engine cooking is a great way to sample regional foods. Think about crayfish in Louisiana (see page 103). Lake perch in Wisconsin. Abalone in northern California (look ahead, if you must, to our abalone recipe, page 118). And think of the fun you could have on vacation, with endless, monotonous rides made bearable by salivating over that dinner cooking right under your own hood. Instead of "When are we going to get there?" the kids will ask, "When will the chicken be done?" Finally, the car-engine chef is using one of the tastiest and most healthful cooking methods, simmering foods in their own juices in a sealed package.

We could go on, maybe even mentioning the conservation benefits of cooking with heat that otherwise would go straight toward melting the ice caps. That's right—every Btu you trap in a veal scallop or pork tenderloin is a Btu that won't go toward submersing Micronesia and hitching the Sun Belt up to Manitoba. But never mind the beneficial side effects. Ever and always, food justifies itself.

2

BEGINNER'S LUCK—AND SKILLS

A half hour in traffic proves that any dolt can drive, but your first experiences in the kitchen no doubt convinced you that it takes at least a marginally able dolt to make dinner.

While we'll assume that you pass muster on that score, there are nevertheless a trunkful of tips and techniques peculiar to car-engine cooking that you must understand before you start dribbling chicken fat down the side of your exhaust manifold. To paraphrase David Byrne, this ain't no Hotpoint, this ain't no micro, this ain't no fooling around. . . .

HERE'S YOUR ENGINE

Like everything else, car engines used to be a lot simpler. There was a straightforward, uncluttered engine block, with a valve cover either on top or off to one side. A carburetor and intake manifold got the fuel-air mixture into the engine, and an exhaust manifold branched to each of the cylinders to carry off the hot, spent gases of combustion. All the other components—distributor, starter, fuel pump, radiator, fan, and so forth—stood out plain and simple. In fact, the single most plentiful thing under your old hood was air. If you were working on your engine in those days and dropped a wrench, it fell through and landed on the ground.

Today, the ground is one thing you *won't* see when you look under the hood. What with power assists for braking and steering, air-conditioning, fuel injection, turbocharging, emission controls, and the electronic paraphernalia that drives you batty with dashboard commands to shift gears at absurdly low RPMs, today's engine compartment looks like an unkempt spare-parts drawer at NASA. As far as things like fuel savings and pollution abatement go, this is all to the good. (If the greenhouse effect turns out to be the real thing and not some computer model gone haywire, you can forget car-engine cooking and just fry eggs on the sidewalk.) But the cluttering of engine compartments with gadgetry has posed a challenge for the cook.

It's frustrating as hell now to find the perfect spot for a package of chicken thighs, only to find it's already taken by the vacuum-assisted pressure sensor for the snibulator pump. We remember reading a story in one car magazine in which a guy described his father's early-fifties technique of securing cans of baked beans to his manifold with baling wire. Aside from the fact that the whole purpose of this book is to take you beyond beans, we defy anyone to find two spots on a modern car engine from which a length of baling wire could be safely secured. For that matter, we defy you to find baling wire, unless your kitchen-on-wheels was manufactured by John Deere.

Still, there is a positive side to this tangle of technology. Inadvertently, it often affords small crannies in which food packages can be wedged tightly (which ties in with the current "portions for one" trend) as well as miles of wiring and tubing that can be used to hold food in place.

But let's throw it into reverse for a second. Despite all these changes—and the fact that many engines are now mounted sideways so they can link up with the transaxle for front-wheel drive—the basic automotive power plant still shares certain elemental design features with its clean-lined forebears. Engines, for instance, are still defined by the number of cylinders they have: in the vast majority of cases, eight, six, or four. The exceptions are the mighty twelve-cylinder Jaguars (now sadly extinct) and BMWs, five-cylinder Audis, and three-banger Third World–mobiles like the old Chevy Sprint. (You can *probably* cook on the motors of this class of vehicles, but only if you find the recipe manual for one of those kiddie ovens that bake brownies with lightbulbs.) Anyway, all of these machines burn fuel—hence the term *internal combustion*—and in the process, all of them get hot.

Ah, but how hot is hot, and what parts get hottest? The first thing we should point out is that we're not talking about "engine temperature" as it is expressed by the idiot light or, if you're lucky, the gauge on your dashboard. Strictly speaking, the dash indicator is giving you the temperature not of the engine but of the coolant circulating between the radiator and the block. If you have a real gauge, the number in the middle, where the needle is supposed to be, is most likely 220; the number up at the end—highlighted in a frantic shade of red—is probably 260. This latter figure is intimately associated with the phenomenon of sweaty guys with their cars pulled over to the side of the Garden State Parkway in August, hoods up and rubbery-smelling steam pouring out into the pure Jersey summer air. You don't ever want to hit 260.

No, we're not talking coolant temperature. What we're interested in is the actual temperature of the exposed metal parts of the engine, surfaces that can be a hell of a lot hotter than the coolant circulating beneath them. We've heard the figure 600 degrees Fahrenheit bandied about (and are willing to believe it as far as the exhaust manifold is concerned), but for our purposes, we don't care as much about numbers as results. If you want to play Mr. Wizard, you could buy a couple of those high-temperature thermometers that people stick on their wood stoves and stovepipes (to tell them when to adjust the dampers) and affix them to different surfaces of your engine. We never bother with this, because (a) it is too troublesome and scientific (our dampers are maladjusted too) and (b) on a modern engine, surfaces are so broken up that your foil-wrapped food is likely to be in contact with several components at once. What we favor is the time-tested method of temperature verification known as "burn your finger." This is simple. Just get your engine up to operating temperature, turn off the ignition, lift the hood, and touch metallic things with your finger until you burn it. Not third-degree, just the kind of quick hit where you pull your hand back fast and stick your finger in your mouth. Forget trying this on any parts made of plastic—there's a lot of it under the hood nowadays—because it will never get hot enough to do anything more than mildly warm things.

Remember, you aren't necessarily looking for the hottest spots. Car-engine cooking is an extremely inexact science, and there is plenty of opportunity to balance fast cooking on a very hot surface with slow cooking on a not-so-hot surface.

Successful engine cooking comes down to these two questions: How far are you driving? and When do you expect to be hungry?

Besides, cooking temperature is just one consideration. You're looking for not only a place that's hot enough, but one that's commodious and secure enough. We'd much rather take an hour longer to cook a package of stuffed eggplant in a large enough cranny that wasn't roaring hot than to jam it into the seventh circle of hell and run the risk of having the foil break or, worse yet, the whole package fall out onto the road. (You try to retrieve an eggplant in traffic, and we're not responsible.)

An inexact science, to be sure. We'd love to be able to tell you what location will cook each dish the best on each and every car engine, but the vast number of differences in engines and related components and in the cooking requirements of various foods makes this impossible. What we can do is offer the accompanying diagrams on basic engine configuration and throw in a few tips on different engine parts—and different cars—that we've had experience with. Read up, then roll up your sleeves and resort to the empirical method.

You've probably noticed that we talk a lot about exhaust manifolds. As we said before, this is the hottest part of the engine surface because it carries the gases that are the waste products of combustion in the cylinders. From here, they go through the muffler to the exhaust pipe, then into the atmosphere to threaten civilization. If you

IT'S NOT MOM'S KITCHEN, BUT . . .

Some car fanciers seem to be awestruck by the sight of a big V-8 nesting in a sea of tubes and hoses. From a culinary point of view, cooking on one of these is like trying to do a seating arrangement in the Collyer brothers' apartment. Just remember, all those doodads are there for a reason. Whether it's good or bad, don't move them if they don't want to go.

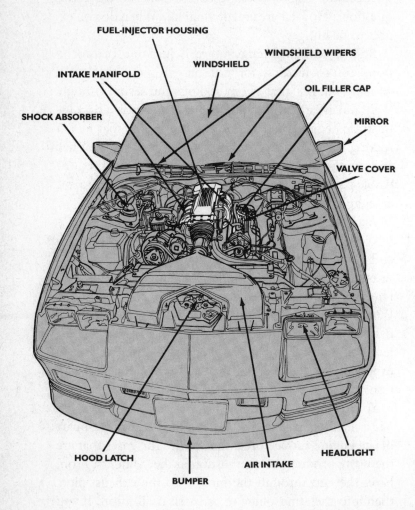

FUEL-INJECTOR HOUSING

WINDSHIELD WIPERS

WINDSHIELD

INTAKE MANIFOLD

OIL FILLER CAP

SHOCK ABSORBER

MIRROR

VALVE COVER

HOOD LATCH

HEADLIGHT

AIR INTAKE

BUMPER

HOT AS IN HOTPOINT

Turbocharging, as on this Chrysler Corporation four-cylinder model, is a popular method of squeaking enough power out of a small engine to satisfy both the EPA and those bozos who think streaks of black rubber point to their manliness. To us, it's just one more oven obstacle.

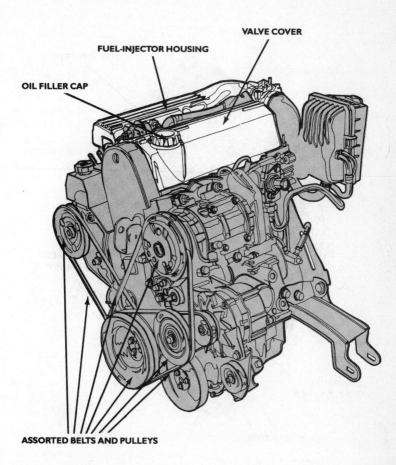

VALVE COVER

FUEL-INJECTOR HOUSING

OIL FILLER CAP

ASSORTED BELTS AND PULLEYS

SMALL ENOUGH FOR A STUDIO

Here's a neat little apartment-size model four-cylinder engine. The fluted valve cover on top will put nice sear lines on your steaks; with a little ingenuity, you should be able to fix a couple of fish fillets on the slanted exhaust manifold guard.

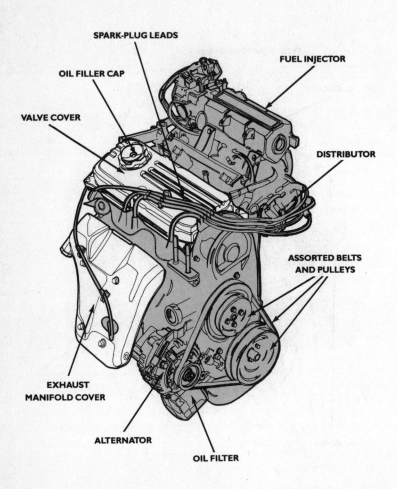

SPARK-PLUG LEADS

FUEL INJECTOR

OIL FILLER CAP

VALVE COVER

DISTRIBUTOR

ASSORTED BELTS
AND PULLEYS

EXHAUST
MANIFOLD COVER

ALTERNATOR

OIL FILTER

have an old car with a fully exposed and easily accessible exhaust manifold (see page 20), you've got a nice, quick cooking surface—provided you have a way to keep food secured to the engine. Modern engines, on which any number of external contraptions obscure much of the manifold, actually often compensate for increased cooking time by providing more nooks and crannies for tucking. If you can't take advantage of direct heat from the manifold, don't despair; just take a longer ride and figure that you're cooking in an oven instead of on a barbecue grill.

Actually, you don't need the exhaust manifold at all. On an old V-8, you should have plenty of space for less intense cooking on top of the engine block itself, alongside the carburetor and beneath the air filter.

> NOTE: When exploring the possibilities of this territory, *never* put anything where it will interfere with the free movement of the accelerator linkage. Also, *never* think you can use the air-filter housing as a warming oven, no matter how much empty space there seems to be in there.

Even smaller cars have their engine-top possibilities—remember, that historic first package of Schwartz's smoked meat was wedged alongside the air filter of a four-cylinder diesel Rabbit.

The best setup we have ever come across for easy-access, top-of-the-engine cooking is the upper surface of the in-line six in a 1965 Jaguar XK-E. If you can think of no other reason to own an E-type Jag—in which case your soul is as dead as a road-kill armadillo—consider that long, uncluttered block, the top of which is formed into a deep V by the slanted valve covers on either side. The plugs come in right at the top, but they hardly inter-

FIVE NO-NOS

1. Interfering with free movement of the accelerator linkage. This is a spring-loaded device that connects the gas pedal with the carburetor or fuel-injection system, thus regulating the flow of fuel to the cylinders. If it jams, either you won't go or you won't stop. *Give it a wide berth.*

2. Blocking the flow of air into the engine's air intake. Internal combustion requires gas and air. *Let your motor breathe.*

3. Indiscriminate yanking on wires, hoses, and so forth to secure food packages. Better you eat at a burger joint than pull out a spark-plug wire. *If the package doesn't fit, don't force it.*

4. Placing, checking, or removing food with the motor running. Being a fan belt means never having to say you're sorry. *Come back with the same number of fingers you started with.*

5. Foil-wrapping foods with too much liquid. Aluminum foil may make a wonderful customized cooking vessel, but a pot it's not. No car owner's manual calls for basting the engine.

fere. This is the place for roasting elongated items like pork tenderloin or eye of the round. What's more, the cooking area is so nicely exposed that you never even have to get grease on your bony, aristocratic knuckles where they poke through the holes on your driving gloves. Until Subaru comes out with an optional *teppanyaki* grill, the Jag gets our convenience award.

Spark plugs can actually be as much of a help as a hindrance. When you find them set into a recess deep enough to require an extension on your socket wrench at tune-up time, you've also found a good spot to insert small, individual items like boned chicken thighs. If the plug recesses are close to the exhaust manifold on one side of the engine, the food placed there will cook faster, so, depending on the recipe, stop along the way and move your packages from one side to the other. Otherwise, you could be embarrassed—as we once were—by baked apples baked only halfway across. (We haven't baked apples since, but feel free to give them a try.)

Fuel injection, now standard on all makes, presents some interesting possibilities. Look under the hood of a new car and you'll see a shiny flat surface, usually made of cast aluminum and about nine or ten inches square, that sits right up top on the middle of the engine. That's the housing for the fuel-injection apparatus. While there are often little niches beneath which you can jam things between the housing and the engine block, what we're really interested in is that griddlelike expanse up top. We first tried it in the Lincoln Town Car we drove in the One Lap of America rally, and were disappointed to find that it was only good for warming precooked things like cured ham steak with a side of baked beans. That shouldn't have surprised us, since the fuel injectors aren't a source of heat, and the housing top is pretty far removed from the fiery innards of the engine. But we reasoned that since a good deal of ambient heat is trapped under the hood, and the housing *is* made of a conductive material, it was worth another try. (After all, Calphalon pots are made of aluminum, aren't they?)

Our faith in the injector housing was vindicated on a drive up the Maine coast in an '88 Chrysler New Yorker.

Atop that flat aluminum surface, we placed two foil packages, each containing a stuffed and partially boned Rock Cornish game hen. After two hours of driving, we opened one package and discovered that the hens were not only cooking, but browning beautifully. We flipped the packages over, got back on the road, and ate the little hens, done to a turn, after only four hours of touring the scenic Maine coast.

We have to offer two caveats regarding fuel-injector–housing cookery. The first involves hood clearance—the gap between cooking surface and hood. If there's too much clearance, your food is going to fall off. And if there isn't enough, you're going to slam down the hood and squash the packages, break the foil, and make what can only be described as a big mess. (The game hens, by the way, flattened just enough, rather like a pressed galantine; this probably helped them cook as well as they did.)

So here's the strategy. Before you put any food on the injector housing, make a cone of aluminum foil about four or five inches high. Put it on the housing and shut the hood. Now lift the hood and see how much the cone has been flattened. Too much? You'll have to cook flat food, like fish fillets. Not very? Then wad some additional foil and place it atop your packages of food to hold them in place. It's that simple.

We said there were two caveats, remember? (Nice attention span. Good thing for you they got rid of leaded gas.) The other one has to do with the weather. When it's really cold outside—say, under 20 degrees Fahrenheit—the moderate heat that you get atop the injector housing often won't do the trick. We remember the time we had to do a car-cooking demo at a winter street fair in the tony Hudson Valley town of Piermont, New York. The pièce de résistance was stuffed boneless chicken breasts,

AN OLD PRO TURNS ON HIS STOVE

An experienced engine chef lovingly places dinner atop the fuel-injector housing on a Pontiac V-6. He's already done the foil-cone test (see page 24) and knows the hood will keep it secure. He also knows enough to keep his bare fingers away from the hot metal.

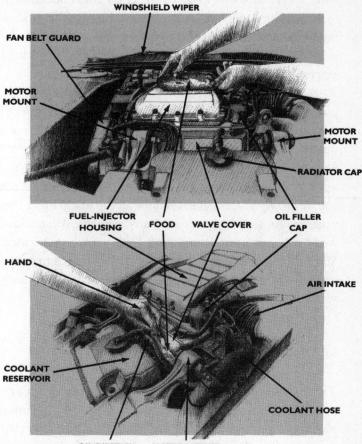

A SMALL PORTION FOR A SMALL DIET

If you've got a small appetite (we don't) and can make do with small portions, there are some bite-size places on the engine available for cooking. Here, our chef wedges an appetizer between the valve cover and the oil dipstick. Wedgies like this are best removed slowly and carefully.

done atop the injectors on an '89 Pontiac Grand Prix—but it was so damned cold that day that even though we'd driven all the way up from Paterson, New Jersey, the chicken wasn't done. (It reminded us of the time on Cape Cod, years ago, when we failed to get the rocks hot enough in a traditional pit-style clambake, and dug up the food to find lobsters that were green on one side and red on the other.) A quick search led us to a toaster oven and a long extension cord, with which we bent the truth a little.

Once in a while, you'll come across a particular model whose designer seems to have been thinking about your needs as a car-engine cook. We once rented an '88 Toyota Camry; we immediately popped the hood to size up the kitchen and discovered, next to the right wheel well, a big square empty space that looked for all the world like a bun warmer. As to what the Toyotans were thinking about when they put a bun warmer in a Camry, we have no idea. Since theirs is a culture that places no great stock in baked goods, we can only assume that this was yet another canny ploy to play to the American market.

WILL IT SMELL FUNNY?

This is not a particularly bright question, but it is asked so often that we may as well finally lay it to rest. The usual phrasing is "Won't the food end up smelling and tasting like oil and gas?" or "Is there any danger from the exhaust?"

Let's put the answer this way. When you check into the Hotel Cipriani in Venice and throw your complimentary terry-cloth bathrobe over the heated towel rack, do you worry about getting it wet? Of course not, because you know the hot water that heats the towels is *inside* the pipes that make up the rack. If it isn't, Cipriani is in big trouble—the same as you are if there's oil or gas sloshing around under your hood outside the proper channels. (If the leak is bad enough to cause serious food contamination, your engine probably won't be running long

A COOK'S COMPARISON
OF EIGHT LATE-MODEL CAR ENGINES

A systematic appraisal of the cooking capabilities of every automotive-engine configuration ever manufactured would be the car chef's equivalent of the *Larousse Gastronomique,* and would doubtless fill as many pages. Such a comprehensive appraisal is obviously outside the scope of this book, but in order to get you thinking about what to look for, we have stuck our heads under the hoods of eight representative 1998 models. A list such as this cannot outline all of the possibilities each engine presents; resourceful road cooks will likely find toasty spots that have slipped, both literally and figuratively, between the cracks in this chart.

And don't forget older models. The title of this book, after all, is derived from the exhaust manifold, and it is on vintage iron that this tubular griddle, lately interred beneath mounds of Flash Gordon plumbing, will most likely show itself. But don't feel bad if you're stuck with a brand-new car. Cooking on and around injector housings (successors to the intake manifolds of yore) and valve covers is a subtle and rewarding art.

MAKE AND MODEL	ENGINE DESIGNATION	FUEL-INJECTOR-HOUSING COOKING SURFACE
Mercedes-Benz ML-320	3.2 liter V-6	$7'' \times 9\frac{1}{2}''$[1]
GMC Suburban SLT	Vortec 7400 V-8	Not accessible[3]
Chevrolet Venture Minivan[5]	3400 V-6	Plastic cover
Oldsmobile Aurora	4.0 liter V-8	Plastic[7] cover
Subaru Forester	2.5 liter 4-cylinder	$5'' \times 20''$[8]
Oldsmobile Cutlass	3100 V-6[11]	$12\frac{1}{2}'' \times 6''$
Chevrolet S-10 pickup truck	2200 4-cylinder	Plastic cover
Range Rover	4.6 liter V-8	$4'' \times 11\frac{1}{2}''$

[1] Nicely interlocking grooves in top, like a giant zipper; perfect for anchoring foil packets.

[2] Finally, a space big enough for a decent-size boned capon.

[3] Most available space around engine is filled with a bird's nest of cables and hoses, all covered in ribbed plastic. Not a good cooker, but then, maybe Suburban drivers are so macho they eat their food raw.

[4] You might be able to heat up a few Pop-Tarts, but not much more.

[5] We like to think we're pretty mechanically adept, but we concluded we'd probably starve while trying to figure how to open the hood on this thing.

[6] Good for small, malleable entrées or big appetizers (see **JB's Mall Pups**, page 88).

[7] The big, silver, space-age-composite panel that covers the top of the Olds flagship looks as inviting as a diner griddle, but it's a big letdown. If only it were cast aluminum, you could idle and make pancakes.

[8] Only good on the left side (i.e., the passenger side—left as you face the engine). Good for molding one fairly large sausage, say, a bauernwurst. Throw one on, invite your friends over, and call it "Axis Night."

[9] One of us owns this car, and we have to say that its engine looks less like an automobile power plant than anything we've ever seen. The upper surfaces have a for-

EXHAUST-MANIFOLD COOKING SURFACE	FOIL-CONE TEST (CLEARANCE BETWEEN HOOD AND UPPERMOST ENGINE SURFACE)	VALVE COVERS	SERVINGS
Not accessible	$5\frac{1}{2}''$ [2]	Not accessible	2
Not accessible	Not applicable	Two $2\frac{1}{2}''$ x 12″ [4]	2
13″ x $4\frac{1}{4}''$ [6]	6″	Not accessible	3
Plastic cover	2″	16″ x $6\frac{1}{2}''$	4 small
Not applicable [9]	Not applicable [10]	Not applicable	2
14″ x 2″ [12]	2″	Not applicable	4
13″ x 6″	$1\frac{1}{4}''$	Not accessible	2 [13]
Not applicable	1″ [14]	3″ x $10\frac{1}{2}''$ [15] (passenger side only)	4

bidding array of moving parts, but there are some promising tuckaway corners underneath. It's so daunting, all in all, that we prefer to keep cooking on the '89 Pontiac Grand Prix purchased with the advance from the first edition of *Manifold Destiny*.

[10] Because the highest points on the engine are by no means cooking surfaces.

[11] An interesting contrast with its upscale cousin, the Aurora. Unlike the Aurora's sleek, plastic-sheathed mill, the Cutlass engine has exposed metal cooking surfaces all over the place. This shows that the rich, ultimately, don't get to have as much fun.

[12] It'd have to be something very malleable, and you'd have to wedge it firmly—the surface slants at a 45-degree angle. We'd call it a recipe for disaster, as in foil-pack fallout.

[13] A good appetizer vehicle. If you want an entrée, go "pick up" some takeout.

[14] One of the lowest cone-test results. Fillet of sole might be possible with little or no foil wedging; make it Dover sole.

[15] For heating mashed potatoes: It is a British car, after all.

enough to cook anything anyway.) As for exhaust, it should come out of the pipe at the back of the car. If it is leaking through faulty plumbing anywhere farther up front, it is likely to get into the passenger compartment and enable you to discuss your next meal with Escoffier himself.

Still, the outer surfaces of a car engine are seldom squeaky-clean, and by "blackened," Paul Prudhomme doesn't mean tainted with crud from a valve cover—aside from what bogus Cajun menus in suburban fern bars may lead you to believe. This is why one of the first rules of car-engine cooking is this: Wrap everything *three times* in aluminum foil. It makes checking for doneness a bit of a pain, but it virtually guarantees a hermetic seal that locks flavor in and dirt out. Remember, *three times*. No more, no less.

FOOD SELECTION AND PRECOOKING PREP WORK

Although the Triple-Foil Wrap rule is the key to successful car-engine cookery, there are a few other dos and don'ts that, when applied with a dose of the plentiful highway commodity called common sense, will assure that things get done properly (or, in cooking terms, properly done).

First off, keep your recipes simple. You'll notice that along with regional variety, simplicity was one of the main criteria in our selection of recipes. This is not because we believe, like the Shakers, that it's a gift to be simple; on the contrary, much of what is really fun and worth doing in this world is, like nature itself, idiotically complex. Gilt lilies are the very stuff of life: We once boned a whole capon, stuffed it with alternating layers of chicken mousseline, duxelles, and spinach soufflé, and wrapped it in brioche. But we had the good sense to cook it in an oven, not on a car engine.

One thing to remember is to avoid recipes that involve a lot of liquid, since this will make the foil packages easier to puncture, and messier if they do. (The only exceptions to this rule are situations involving cans or semirigid containers, and engines—such as classic unadorned flatheads, or the power plant on a Greyhound bus—that can accommodate them.) Also, you're better off if the foods you wrap can be contoured against hot parts of the engine, preferably with the bulky foil seam on the outside, for better contact and heat distribution. (See sidebar below.) Don't use cuts of meat, fish, or poultry that are too thick. And bones, if left in, will make packages too rigid—as well as increase cooking time.

There isn't much to be said about food placement that wasn't already covered when we talked about engine configuration. When they designed your car engine, they also designed its available cooking surfaces, and what you see is what you get. Keep in mind, though, that you can com-

WRAPPING TECHNIQUES AND ALUMINUM-FOIL BRAND COMPARISONS

We've all wrapped our share of leftovers.

Bundling up meals for engine cooking is a similar procedure, only more precise—like wrapping Christmas presents. First, make sure nothing you're wrapping is going to poke through the foil (chicken-wing tips can do this). If you spot potential trouble, wrap the pointy parts loosely, wadding foil as necessary to provide a cushion on the innermost foil layer; the two subsequent layers can be wrapped more snugly. Second, leave enough foil on the sides to make a secure, overlapping fold. (Use extra-wide foil if necessary.) Bring the foil up around the top of the food and make a flat, interlocking seam, like the ones on a pair of good blue jeans, and tuck the excess underneath on both sides. You might try alternating the direction of the seams (top to bottom) on each successive wrapping, but if all your seams run on top of each other, be sure to put the seamless side of your package against the engine for better heat distribution.

You'll notice that we haven't recommended heavy-duty foil. Try it if you want; we find it behaves no better than the standard variety. As for whether to put the shiny or matte-finish side out, we feel it makes no difference. The shiny surface does make for a better display, though, when you're showing off to your friends.

Last but not least, be careful when unwrapping, since you may want to rewrap to continue cooking. All aluminum foils become brittle when heated, as heat rearranges the molecules in their crystalline structures into a more orderly pattern.

Here are the results of tests we have had performed on four popular brands of aluminum foil. The purchases were made in Providence, Rhode Island.

BRAND NAME[1]	THICKNESS[2]	PRICE PER 75 SQ. FT.[3]	GOOD HOUSEKEEPING SEAL	STRUCTURAL INTEGRITY	SHINY SURFACE	KOSHER?[4]
Sun Glory	.0004 in.	$1.39	No	None	Mirrorlike	Ⓚ
Stop & Shop	.00045	1.49	No	Acceptable (that .00005 makes a difference)	Slight brushing	Ⓚ
Star	.0006	1.62	No	Pretty good	Pronounced parallel brushing running lengthwise	Ⓤ
Reynolds	.0006	1.79	Yes	Best; stays unwrinkled	Same as Star	Ⓤ

[1] All packages have double-edged cutting bar attached to the box. This appears to be an industry standard.

[2] All thickness figures represent an average of multiple measurements.

[3] Prices may vary.

[4] We have no idea of the religious attributes of aluminum foil.

ALL WRAPPED UP
What can we say about wrapping with tinfoil? We can say: Do it neatly, do it tightly, do it thrice.

HANDS

FOOD

FOIL

CRIMP

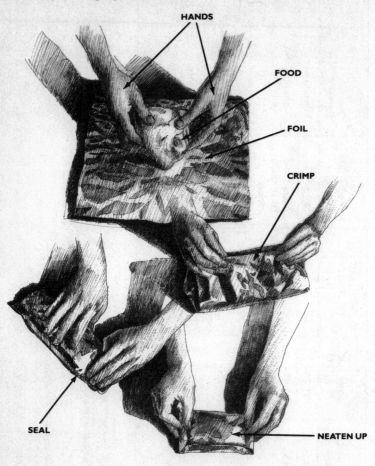

SEAL

NEATEN UP

Step 1—Place food in center of sheet of foil.

Step 2—Pulling foil snugly against your lunch, crimp tightly to make a good seal.

Step 3—Fold ends toward center of package and crimp again.

Step 4—Neaten up by pressing foil into a snug package with no protruding flaps to catch and tear during cooking.
Repeat two more times so food is securely wrapped in three layers of foil.

FIND THAT ROLLS!

Consider the phantom 1920s Rolls-Royce, a car we heard about from a curbside well-wisher in Manitou Springs, Colorado, when we stopped for lunch during the big rally. This guy was watching us conduct a fuel-injector-housing foil-cone test (while at lunch, plan for dinner), and told us that he had heard of a Jazz Age Rolls that had had a little oven cast right into the engine block. A special touring model, he said it was. Did this wonderful car ever exist? And if it did, was it one of a kind or an extremely limited production model? Why wouldn't the PR people at Rolls talk with us when we called them? Why, if what they were trying to come up with was a Toyota-style bun warmer, didn't they call this edition a Buns-Royce? Why would they do that, when "Buns-Royce" sounds like a dancer at Chippendale's? Why is there being rather than nothingness?

Ask questions, son, it's the only way you'll learn anything.

pensate for lack of direct heat by increasing cooking time, or for excessive heat by decreasing cooking time. We found that boned chicken thighs, for example, cook just as nicely on the exhaust manifold of an Olds Cutlass as on the fuel-injector housing of an old Dodge 600. The only difference is that you have to drive the Dodge twice as far.

When you do decide on a surface to use, watch out for sharp protuberances that might puncture your foil wrapping. Little nubs and knurls can be handy, though.

We've had some success with wrapping packages so that excess foil at the ends can be used as tabs to twist around protruding parts, thus holding the food in place. Use what you can find: the oil dipstick, the narrow tubing associated with the emissions-control system, you name it. Just don't run your tabs across too wide a gap—aluminum foil ain't baling wire.

So much for the mechanical angle. The remainder of what there is to be learned about car-engine cuisine has to do with how food behaves, and with the different modes of cooking and the foods to which they are best suited.

Forget boiling. At first, you might think that a car engine is a great place to boil things, because there's no way you can watch the pot. But think about it: Even if you found a hot enough spot on the motor, and a cooking vessel that would fit it, you'd have about as much success boiling something in there as Chrysler did putting record players in the glove compartments of '57 DeSotos. (Don't laugh; they tried it.) You'd leave a trail of soup, even on the smoothest roads.

Likewise, don't think you can roast anything to a crispy stage of doneness—the best you can hope for is a nice browning, as we got with the game hens on the injector housing of the Chrysler New Yorker. This you try to accomplish by minimizing the liquid in your recipe, or keeping it on the engine long enough and in a hot enough spot for the liquid to cook away and leave the surfaces to brown.

What you *can* do nicely is braise foods—cook them gently in a small amount of liquid, just enough to transfer the heat and serve as a vehicle for seasonings. This is where wine comes in handy, as in our recipe for **Poached Fish Pontiac** (page 115)—but remember to keep that

opened bottle in the trunk. When you're working with something delicate, like fish fillets or veal, also be sure to rub the inside of your innermost sheet of foil with plenty of butter or oil to prevent sticking.

Then there's a whole class of apparently simple low-rent dishes that at first glance seem made for car-engine cooking, but that we emphatically do not recommend. We hadn't really thought about grilled cheese, for instance, until we ran across a piece in *The New York Times* about an unnamed "famous and rich performer" who, while traveling the world and staying in swank hotels, always carries a roll of aluminum foil and a clothes iron. Upon arriving in a city before a performance, she heads for the nearest food store and picks up some cheese and a loaf of bread. She makes cheese sandwiches, wraps them in the foil, and cooks them under the iron in her hotel room.

This goofy maneuver presents a certain dilemma. On the one hand, it's pretty tacky and takes advantage of a free energy source (the hotel's electricity), and on those counts we're in favor of it. But there are two drawbacks. First, the bread and cheese you're likely to pick up at five-thirty on a Sunday afternoon in Moscow, Idaho, probably won't be the kind you'd really want to eat. It would be a lot simpler to just get something like a Stewart System Styrofoam-and-cheese concoction and let some sleazy bartender heat it in the micro. After all, your travel iron probably doesn't serve drafts.

The second drawback is that room service, especially in the best hotels (we're assuming that you're not always traveling through places like Moscow, Idaho), is one of the crowning glories of Western civilization. If you can pick up the phone, press one button, and cause food and drink to magically appear at your door, why bother burning your fingers heating bad cheese and white bread into an indistinguishable colorless mass under an iron that you have to lug all over the place?

Or on your car engine? One of the points in favor of engine cooking is that it allows you to enjoy good food that you've made yourself using good ingredients. If you're just going to start heating and melting, you're only slumming, like Ms. Famous-and-Rich.

At the other end of the spectrum, there are the fad cooking techniques. The Westin Hotel in Calgary, Alberta, for instance, used to flog a new gimmick called "hot-rock cooking." According to the pop-up folder they put on the night table in your room, it's "the latest European restaurant trend—cooking your own food on a hot rock at your table" (the one in the restaurant downstairs, not the one by your bed). Neither of us got to try this silly business on our last pass through Calgary, but it occurred to us that this "latest trend" is really nothing more than a pedestrian version of engine cooking. The big difference is, when you're done cooking on your hot rock, you're still in Calgary, while if you had fixed a nice veal cutlet on your engine, you'd be up in the mountains heading for Lake Louise by the time it was done.

Still, for those of you who can't resist a new craze, we have accommodated the hot-rock idea to car-engine cookery. First, wedge the biggest rock you can up against your exhaust manifold. Drive for about a week to get it hot (depending on the direction you take, you might still be in Alberta if you start out in Calgary). Now stop your car, slap some food on the rock—unwrapped—and wait for the edges to curl.

A word of warning: There's some odd food up in the Canadian home of hot-rock cooking. At the same Westin, the breakfast menu was hawking low-cholesterol artificial eggs for omelets. When asked if the eggs came from artificial chickens, the waitress replied, "No, they're from Dome Petroleum."

TIMING, EQUIPMENT, AND SAFETY

When you set out to learn how to cook the way normal people do, all you have to do is master the ways in which different foods react to different treatments and temperatures—for example, the ability of egg whites to expand and hold air, the tendency of cream sauces containing egg to curdle if you get them too hot, and the fact that you can panfry a steak better in cast iron than in stainless steel painted with a token wash of copper. You don't have to go to the Cordon Bleu to learn these things, but if you do, you can write a serious cookbook renouncing everything you were taught and yammering about how Western cuisine should be influenced by the dietary predilections of the !Kung Bushmen of Namibia.

You don't have to study under a despot in a *toque blanche* to learn car-engine cooking either, but it will help if you remember that you'll be dealing with the peculiarities not only of different foods, but of different engines. Nowhere does this come across more clearly than in the matter of timing. When we suggest times in our recipes, don't take us too seriously—and likewise, don't follow your own recipes chapter and verse when it comes to converting and timing them for use on the old V-6. *Experiment.* Something that took us four hours may take you two if you have access to a hotter part of the engine. Or the reverse may be true. About the only general rule we can lay down is that dishes almost always take longer to cook on a car engine than they do on a stove. Like we said, it's an inexact science. Relax and enjoy the scenery.

The downside to learning how to work a particular, beloved automobile engine like a six-burner Viking is that you'll hate like hell to sell the car. The only consolation is that when you run the ad in the paper, you can throw in a come-on phrase such as "Cooks like a champ."

When we first wrote *Manifold Destiny,* we hoped that eventually onboard computers would come to the aid of car chefs. In those days, it looked as if more and more cars were going to be equipped with computers that could tell you the gas mileage you were getting at any given moment and how far you could go on the gas you had. By now, these gizmos could have been set up so you could program them with the pertinent data—what you were making and where on the engine you had put it—and they would tell you how long it was going to take to cook and where, at any given speed, you would be when dinner was done. But the computers never really took off, probably because nobody gives a damn about gas mileage anymore. If there's a computer in the dash nowadays, it's there so you can check your E-mail in traffic or call up a street map of Utica, New York.

Maybe some offshoot of the new "On-Star" system will do the trick. You know On-Star—it's the satellite link that alerts the Strategic Air Command, or Ernie's Texaco, or somebody, when your air bag goes off and pins you in so you can't dial your cell phone. Well, picture it configured so you could give the relevant recipe information to the satellite, then sit back and let the satellite tell you when dinner was ready to eat. This would be cheaper than the Hubble Space Telescope, and it wouldn't send back depressing pictures of whole galaxies blowing up . . . as if we didn't live in one ourselves, for God's sake.

At this point we should address the issue of rareness and doneness, which relates to the latest installment in the "Fear of Food" movement that has sprung up since the first edition of *Manifold Destiny* came out. Like a lot of other reckless souls, we like meat that hasn't been cremated to a uniform shade of gray throughout. (We know, we know . . . the FDA says to cook it gray all the way through.) We should point out that most of the problems with contaminated meat have involved hamburger, which isn't recommended for car-engine cookery anyway (although we like this rare too, preferring to grind our own if it comes down to that). But if it makes you feel any better, just drive farther. Far be it from us to get in the way of the government telling you how to eat.

The equipment requirements for car-engine cooking are minimal. It helps to have an oven mitt or two, though there's nothing wrong with the old gloves you keep under the seat for shoveling snow and changing tires. It

would be nice to mount a paper-towel dispenser under your dashboard, and maybe another for aluminum foil— it pays to keep extra foil on hand, so you can rewrap food after you tear the foil when checking to see if it's done. Beyond these basics, there exists the unexplored realm of specialty cooking equipment made only for use on car engines. We'd love to see a pot manufacturer come out with a line of covered vessels made to fit securely in the larger under-hood crevices of popular models—if for no other reason than the sheer pleasure of walking into a kitchen-gadget shop with a name like The Blue Nantucket Turnip and asking for a saucepan to fit a '96 Isuzu Trooper. Or maybe auto-parts stores could sell them. Our other dream gadget is a lasagna pan that would slide into special flanges attached to the underside of the hood. (We can't figure out how this would work, though, without dumping tomato sauce onto the windshield wipers.)

A KIT FOR THE CAR KITCHEN

If the Scout motto "Be prepared" remains a guiding principle in your life, you probably have stashed in your trunk a road emergency kit containing car-repair tools, a flashlight, spare fuses, flares, an ice scraper, and so forth. Why not be prepared for impromptu engine cooking as well? You never know when you'll pass a grocery store running a special on pork tenderloins.

In addition to an ample supply of aluminum foil and paper towels, here are some essential items with which the rolling kitchen ought to be equipped. Feel free to elaborate or simplify to the extent of your own ambition; what we've listed will see you through most of the recipes in this book.

—Eating utensils and plastic plates. If it won't make your car look ridiculous, carry one of those Edwardian baskets containing a Royal Doulton Service for twelve.

—Small cutting board. Plastic is better than wood, since you probably won't be cleaning it right away. Wood retains bacteria if you don't scrub it pronto—that's why all those commercial butcher blocks wound up in trendy antique shops. Even if you do use plastic, wash it after every outing—especially if you've been cutting raw meat.

—A couple of sharp knives. A French chef's knife and a boning knife should cover all situations.

—Mixing bowl, two quarts at the most.

—Metal spoon for mixing. Wooden spoons are nice, but they present the same problem as the cutting board (see above).

—Plastic measuring cup.

—Pounding mallet. If you get one made out of rubber, you can also use it to knock out minor dents.

—Salt, pepper, and assorted spices: Pick out the ones you use most frequently. A plastic squeeze bottle full of cooking oil isn't a bad idea, but we wouldn't want to store it in a hot trunk too long.

—Rubber gloves for handling the occasional hot pepper, when you can't wash your hands right away.

—Can opener.

—Oven mitt(s).

Remember, again, these critical safety tips: *Stay away from the accelerator linkage.* Don't move, remove, or block anything crucial to the car's operation. Always shut the engine off when you put food in to cook, and when you check to see if it's done. Avoid moving parts in general, especially pulleys, belts, and the radiator fan. (Get your fingers near that fan, and your car engine will become a food processor rather than a stove.)

PRACTICE RUNS: A COUPLE OF EASY FOOD CATEGORIES THAT WILL BREAK YOU IN AS A CAR-ENGINE COOK

For all our disparagement of the heat-a-can school of car-engine cookery, we nevertheless remember our roots at Schwartz's and also recognize that some timid souls will be looking for a way to ease into this wonderful new technology. Here, then, are a few tips on what we call the "ready-made" and "ready-bought" categories of food.

Around 1920, the Dadaist artist Marcel Duchamp shook up the world of aesthetics by attaching manufactured items such as snow shovels and porcelain urinals to gallery walls and calling the result art. Ready-made art, to be precise. Nowadays, the giant food-processing companies, using supermarkets as their galleries, have taken a page out of Duchamp's book and offered us a vast array of ready-made food. It's manufactured, to be sure, and it can inspire the same sort of arguments as the stuff Duchamp put on display. Was that art? Is this food?

For better or worse, it's possible to pull off the highway into a supermarket lot anywhere in America and come out with something marginally resembling dinner—just heat on your engine and serve. The basic choices are to be found in either the canned-goods or frozen-food sections. These suggestions are presented only for rank beginners and those in dire need of a car-cooked food fix; they involve about as much creative thought as trying to figure out whether to turn right into the Taco Bell or left into Denny's.

Canned goods fall into two categories—liquid-packed, and semisolid mush. The first group includes such items as green beans, baby peas, Irish potatoes, and stewed tomatoes. The second takes in such crowd pleasers as corned-beef hash, baked beans, and dog food. For the automotive chef, the cooking methods are the same for either category. Remove the label, punch a couple of small vent holes in the lid, cover lightly with a square of foil, and find a place—preferably on or close to the manifold—that allows as much direct contact with the can as possible. If simple wedging will not secure the can, perhaps shims of crumpled foil with help. (If you insist on being a classicist, try baling or picture-hanging wire.) The liquid-packed items will cook somewhat faster; if you overcook any of these, they'll just be even mushier than usual. If you overdo something like hash, you'll get some crustiness around the edges, but this might actually improve the texture. At any rate, make sure the cans are securely in place and drive until steam comes out of the vents—maybe forty-five minutes to an hour for the average fifteen-ounce can.

Do not, under *any* circumstances, try this procedure without punching the vent holes. Without them, a can could explode under your hood. Even if it doesn't, you could still be in a lot of trouble. Just as the temperature of your antifreeze can rise above its boiling point because the system is sealed, so can an unvented cartridge of SpaghettiOs get a lot hotter than 212 degrees Fahrenheit. Remember the whooshing fountain you got last time you popped the cap on an overheated radiator before letting it cool? Imagine that fountain being full of superheated, sticky pasta, which will stick to you, and tin-can shards, which will stick *into* you. We can give pretty close to a money-back guarantee this is what you'll get if you don't vent cans before heating. *Be warned!*

On the foolproof side, but showing no more imagination, are frozen foods. Just pick out your favorite, and shove it under the hood. Heating will take considerably less time if you defrost foods first, though this is best done in a refrigerator to prevent spoilage. Even with that, you may run into problems with sogginess when you predefrost. Not for nothing do the packages tell you, "Do not thaw before cooking." In any event, try to use some common sense: A small frozen loaf of garlic bread covers the business zone of most car engines a lot better than a twelve-inch frozen pizza. If you're using old-fashioned frozen food, the aluminum packaging may already be in place (e.g., TV dinners); just wrap in an outer layer of foil and you're all set. If it's packaged for the microwave, rewrap it entirely in foil. Boiling bags are not recommended.

Obvious suggestions (virtually everything about frozen food is obvious) include shoving enchiladas or fish fillets between fuel-injection intake ports and jamming a Swiss-steak dinner on top of a manifold. Just remember that less-than-solid foods slip and slide. Try to cook a pizza vertically and you'll wind up with a dough disk rising majestically from a swamp of tomato puree and mozzarella. However, frozen peas loosely wrapped can be made to fit just about anywhere. Cooking times will range from about thirty minutes for loose vegetables to two hours or more for some of the beefier entrées.

Ready-boughts are a subject much closer to our hearts. The big difference between ready-mades and ready-

IF YOU INSIST ON COOKING
READY-MADES . . .

As you may have gathered, we are not terribly enthusiastic about cooking off-the-shelf or "ready-made" foods on car engines. For one thing, they're too easy: How can you derive any sense of accomplishment from merely raising the temperature of something that's already been cooked in an industrial vat in Camden, New Jersey? For another, the realm of ready-mades has been getting shabbier and shabbier of late. Once there were just canned foods and frozen vegetables, but during the 1980s, the TV dinner crossbred with the microwave oven and strange new creatures were hatched. Super-markets now devote entire freezers to bizarre vegetable-pasta–cheese sauce concoctions that can be either boiled in the bag or zapped in the micro, and "pocket" meals based on pita bread, croissants, and turnover dough. The vast ma-jority of these things are designed to be micro-waved while they're still frozen, and many are not suitable for the gentle heating a car engine offers even if you do take them out of their plas-tic bags, defrost partially or completely (see page 47), and foil-wrap them. But if you must cook the already cooked, there are a few stand-bys that always do well under the hood. Here are our choices:

— Hot dogs, knockwurst, kielbasa, and the whole family of precooked sausage products you'll find in the shrink-wrap section of your supermarket meat cooler. These have the advantage of cooking fast, and of being dispersible throughout the engine compartment should conditions so dictate. Best of all, they can be mixed and matched with two of the basic food groups . . .

—Sauerkraut and baked beans! In popular folklore, canned beans are usually depicted as the original car-cooked food. As we've mentioned, though, finding room for cans in today's engine-compartment environment is a chancy business. (B&M's seven-ounce size opens up the most possibilities.) The modern way to cook beans in transit is to empty a can into a foil packet, starting with a double thickness of foil to prevent tearing when you bring the sides up for wrapping. You can pop in a few frankfurters, whole or in chunks, and customize the package to fit just about anywhere—just be careful of sharp objects. The same goes for kraut. Either cook it separately, transferred from a plastic bag or can into foil, or make up a *choucroute garnie* that includes your favorite precooked wurst. Just drive until it's all heated through, usually an hour at most.

—Spam, and its cousins in the world of monosyllabic meat products. Spam has lost its allure for many of us who once loved it in the campfire days of childhood, but it does have the advantage of heating quickly, either whole (an engine Spam roast) or in individually wrapped slices tucked against engine hot spots for that fried effect. Just plork it out of its can, and get the foil.

—Corned-beef hash. As malleable as baked beans but not as prone to leakage, hash is at its car-cooked best when you spread it into a flat foil package and do it up brown atop an injector housing that gets fairly hot. Foil-wedge for security, and turn once for uniform crisping. Now if only you could poach an egg somehow . . .

—Little canned hams. Back in the fifties, we thought these were the only things they made behind the Iron Curtain besides atom bombs. These Polish exports are still on the shelves, often in sizes small enough for engine cooking. As with Spam, all you have to do is de-can, foil-wrap either whole or in slices, and slip it onto the old mill.

boughts is individuality, and the intensity of the maker's intent. A good automotive analogy might be the difference between a so-called Indy Pace Car and a low-rider bopping down the bad end of Sunset Boulevard. Detroit pounds out a limited number of Pace Cars; the number is limited by how many saps will shell out several grand extra for the lettering on the side. (The first time we saw a "Pace Car," we almost believed it. Then we thought, "What's it doing on Route 9 in Worcester, Massachusetts?")

A low-rider, on the other hand, is one of a kind. Someone makes it for himself, not particularly caring that BMW owners will chuckle at it condescendingly or that every third cop will pull him over if business is slow that day. One person decides how high the lifts will go, how purple the flocking will be. *He* decides how many dice will hang from the mirror, how many pictures of his mother will be painted on the doors. It's his car, and tough nuts to the rest of the world.

Food is the same way. Stouffer makes its stuffed chicken breasts according to a recipe calculated to offend the fewest number of potential eaters. Oregano? Too spicy for Minneapolis. Real provolone? Too ethnic for Memphis. Thyme? No, someone in Phoenix might realize it doesn't take that much time to do it yourself. It's like the Indy Pace Car: Make it seem distinctive, but keep it palatable to as many people as possible.

Now put those glaciated chicken breasts aside, and step into Tony's Delicatessen on 204th Street in The Bronx. (You can tell you're in the presence of an original, as Tony is an Italian running a traditionally Jewish business in a heavily Irish neighborhood.) Walk up to the display case and gaze at the potato logs. They're cylinders of mashed potatoes, rolled in bread crumbs and deep-fried, fifty cents each. Next to the logs, in keeping with the axle-and-wheel motif, are corned-beef *doughnuts*! These are made of finely ground corned beef, pressed into doughnut shapes, crumbed, and also deep-fried. Seventy-five cents apiece.

Why on earth would anyone make doughnuts out of corned beef? They're heavy as hell, and oily enough to require an EPA variance on the Arctic tundra. On the other hand, why not? Tony makes them and Tony likes them and that's good enough for Tony. Financially, it's a little better for Tony if you buy a few, but he doesn't really care. You're already in the deli, so you'll probably buy something. Who cares if it's a corned-beef doughnut or a meatball hero? Not Tony. Tony would like lowriders if he lived in east L.A.

Ready-boughts make for a marriage of two American ideals, freedom of choice and automobiles, and they are a natural for novice car-engine cooks. You could hop in your car and eat Tony's corned-beef doughnuts straight from the store, of course, but your hands would get so greasy that you'd lose control of your car on the Hutchinson River Parkway. The answer? Wrap 'em in foil, stick 'em on the manifold, and stop at the Mobil station near Mamaroneck to chow down. Just bring plenty of napkins.

A FEW OF OUR FAVORITE READY-BOUGHTS

Finding a great ready-bought is like driving east on Manhattan's Fifty-seventh Street on a late-June morning and watching the sun come up over the East River. (If this doesn't give you a sense of being present at the Creation, you may as well hire a chauffeur and ride around slouched in the backseat with your eyes closed.) Discovery is what life is all about, even if it's only a greasy morsel to pop into your maw.

Here are a few of the morsels we've discovered:
—Corned-beef doughnuts. Even if you're one of the many enemies of the mighty Yankees, there's still a reason to visit The Bronx. These leaden lunches are a sublime melding of a form and a function that have nothing to do with each other—yet in this incarnation, corned beef and doughnuts both make their leap at immortality.
—Piroshki. Bastardized spellings are always a good clue that ready-boughts are nearby. Stop in a little grocery on Russian Hill in San Francisco and check the stock. Take your pick

of cheese, meat, or potato wrapped in a huge hunk of dough the size of a (*ghaack!*) McDonald's burger.

—Deviled crabs. The Hampton, Virginia, restaurant was nothing more than two house trailers stuck together, located about a block from where the excursion boats leave for tours of the Atlantic fleet's mooring in Norfolk. Hampton may not have a lot to offer besides easy parking and cheap crabs, but what more do you need? Pick up a couple, rewrap in foil (keep the crabs in their little aluminum pans for form and crispiness), and let 'em roast.

—Cornish pasties. These delicacies from the Upper Peninsula of Michigan may be a precursor of the idea of boil-in-the-bag meals, except you get to eat the bag. A hefty lunch of cubed meat, potatoes, and vegetables packed into a crescent (not a *croissant*) of stiff dough, it's perfect for munching while you're looking for grasshoppers in Nick Adams's dream fields along the Big Two-Hearted River.

—Coiled bologna. Gallon jars filled with a tight spiral of sausage look like a page out of *Gray's Anatomy.* They're handy because you can cut chunks customized to fit the nooks and crannies of your engine (not to be confused with the ignition coil).

—Stuffed peppers. Cruise the backwater towns of north Jersey until you find an Italian deli that stuffs its own peppers. You're looking for a bread stuffing heavy on the oil and garlic, something with the mean density of

plutonium. The beauty of these is that you can drive from Paterson to Atlantic City with a couple of them on the engine and they won't get soggy. How could they? If they're made right, they already are soggy.
—Meatball on a half-pizza. Another Jersey delight. The "pizza" here is not the ubiquitous tomato pie, but a flat, round bread that splits neatly for stuffing—sort of like Middle Eastern pita, but thicker and breadier. If your meatball sandwich takes up a whole pizza bread, it's a "meatball wheel" (terminology courtesy Sterling's Delicatessen, West Side Avenue, Jersey City).

Ready-boughts are the forgotten flip side of the regional-cuisine trend, and places like Tony's and Schwartz's have their counterparts everywhere. In Kentucky, many small taverns serve rolled oysters—behemoth bivalves rolled and stuffed with cracker crumbs to the point of being a large bulge of cracker moistened with essence of oyster. In Rhode Island, the Shore Dinner Hall at the Rocky Point Amusement Park sells "clam cakes," balls of deep-fried dough studded with chunks of chopped clam. Going to Buffalo? Pass up the chicken wings and stop for some beef on weck, thinly sliced beef sandwiched into a sweetish caraway-seed roll. The list goes on and on: deviled crabs in Newport News, molded onto a thin piece of aluminum that will create a nice crusty bottom when it heats up. Coiled bologna (see sidebar, above) is a North Carolina specialty. Whenever you get peckish, just heat up about eight inches and keep driving. And don't forget the inspiration for *Manifold*

Destiny—smoked meat cut from the brisket at Schwartz's or any of the lesser lights among Montreal's delicatessens. All of these delightful ready-boughts are out there waiting to be wrapped in foil and savored on the road. There may never be a Northwest Passage, but there are still a lot of things in America worth discovering.

3

CAR-ENGINE RECIPES:
FOUR AMERICAN REGIONAL CUISINES

America's penchant for regional cuisines goes far beyond ready-boughts. Just when we thought the fast-food chains and the frozen-diet-dinner makers were about to do to our palates what broadcasting did to our ear for dialects, along came "American Regional." At its best, this trend has sparked a revival of the dishes your mother used to make—if her family had lived in the same place for two hundred years. At its worst, it's inspired blackened cheeseburgers and a California cuisine that can be the gastronomic equivalent of New Age music. And since we first wrote *Manifold Destiny,* the trend has been compounded with what's known as "fusion" cookery, which combines ingredients and techniques from countries that used to know enough to stay the hell away from each other, unless one of them was in urgent need of rubber or silk or tea. As far as American cuisine goes, the more exotic influences still tend to stick to the coast—although any day now, we expect to hear about some place in

Rhinelander, Wisconsin, that does Vietnamese sauer-braten with ginger-potato dumplings.

We've chosen to arrange our favorite recipes geographically. We like to think that this way, they are not only true to the spirit and ingredients of the regions that they represent, but also to the ambiance of automobile travel in those places. What more perfect combination of experiences could there be than to toodle along the rockbound coast of Maine with a cod poaching under your hood? (No, not a lobster. The little buggers crawl around and get caught in the fan belt.)

We've focused our attention on four regions: the Northeast, the Midwest, the South, and California. In addition, we've included a new International section, with a sampling of dishes that have probably already turned up in your hometown but are still foreign enough to give us a chance to blather on about how well traveled we are.

A few words about cooking times: In the recipes that follow, we've begun each recipe with a recommended mileage figure. Keeping in mind what we said earlier about time being a far more important factor than distance in car-engine cooking, we hasten to point out that our recipe mileage numbers are based upon an average speed of 55 mph. Thus, a 110-mile recipe will take two hours to cook. (We know that you can now do 65 legally on most interstates, but we left the double-nickel formula intact because we figure you'll get slowed down by something along the way. As for Montana, where there is a widely disregarded speed limit, you'll have to figure it out for yourself. Have fun out there on the cowboy autobahn!)

Finally, a note about storage before cooking. If you're leaving on a four-hour trip and you're planning to cook a two-hour dish, you'll want to keep your prewrapped food cool until it's time to put it on the engine. Unless it's wintertime and you're using your trunk as a fridge, bring a small cooler to keep perishables from spoiling in transit. If you have a really long haul ahead of you, you may even wish to freeze meals in advance, as we did on the rally. Attempt this only if you have a properly insulated cooler and plenty of ice—and cook your meals immediately after thawing to prevent spoilage. We're not responsible for food poisoning due to improper refrigeration; consult a comprehensive cookbook or home-economics manual for the details of freezing and thawing.

THE NORTHEAST

The Northeast, by our definition, takes in the New England and Middle Atlantic states. New England is where American cookery was born, and where it first acquired the simplicity, honesty, and hearty wholesomeness that have often, in the years since, degenerated into blandness. We have a theory that this downhill slide parallels that of the native English stock, who originally must have been an interesting and adventuresome lot despite their wacky religion, but who have long since settled back to clip coupons while wearing high-water pants with whales embroidered on them. But the best New England cuisine is still mighty satisfying, especially when it is based on the region's abundance of fresh seafood. This is a big plus for the car-engine cook, since fish cooks more quickly than anything else on the old motor. Besides, if you can find enough room under your hood to heat up a can as well as a foil-wrapped fish, you can drive into Boston paying simultaneous tribute to the bean *and* the cod.

New England may be white-bread America, but far-

ther south in the Middle Atlantic states, white bread is more likely to have a real crust. This region's greatest contribution to American gastronomy has been Italian food, to which we pay homage in these pages. If you can cook it on an Italian car, congratulations—unless you still have a Fiat. A more realistic way to get into the spirit of Italian-American highway cookery is to tuck your foil-wrapped treats under the hood of a big white Caddy or a Lincoln Town Car, pop Ol' Blue Eyes into the tape deck, and head out onto the Jersey Turnpike to do it Your Way.

> NOTE: Because the Northeast has the most congested highways in the country, it is very important that you think in terms of time rather than distance when you are car-cooking up this way.

Hit I-84 through Hartford at rush hour, and you could do a whole stuffed fish in the space of three exit ramps.

So, let's eat.

Cutlass Cod Supreme

Cod, the "sacred fish" of New England, is the foundation of the region's vaunted white cuisine. (Note that in the second version of this recipe, we have gotten risqué by adding two ingredients that actually have color—tarragon and paprika.)

Here's the basic version, which is a nice introductory recipe for car-cooking novices. It has all of three ingredients, and it's ready in a jiffy. What's more, it's ideal for impulsive eaters who like to be able to cruise up to the supermarket, breeze through the express lane, and put together their dinner right in the parking lot with no home prep work necessary.

DISTANCE: 40–70 MILES

4 tablespoons butter
4 cod fillets
1 tablespoon lemon juice

At home or on the road, using 1 or 2 tablespoons of the butter, grease 4 separate sheets of foil. Place a cod fillet on each sheet, dot with the remaining butter, and sprinkle with the lemon juice. Wrap each fillet separately.

Cook 45 minutes to 1 hour and 15 minutes, depending on the thickness of the fillets and the location on the car engine.

If you want to get a little fancier and do some advance preparation in your kitchen, try this next version.

To the above ingredients, add:

2 tablespoons butter
1 small onion, very finely minced
1 1/2 teaspoons tarragon
Paprika to taste

At home, melt the butter and add the onion, lemon juice, and tarragon. Arrange each fillet on a separate piece of foil, and brush both sides liberally with the butter mixture. Dust with paprika and wrap.

Cook as on page 62.

Hyundai Halibut with Fennel

New England fishermen used to call big halibut "door-mats." For this recipe, get your steaks cut from one that looks more like a floor mat.

DISTANCE: 55–85 MILES

4 halibut steaks
1 teaspoon oregano
Grated rind of 2 lemons
1 clove garlic, minced
2 fennel bulbs, thinly sliced
Dry vermouth or white wine

At home or on the road, lay the halibut steaks on 4 pieces of buttered foil. Sprinkle each with the oregano, lemon rind, and garlic. Add a generous layer of fennel slices and sprinkle with vermouth or wine. Wrap tightly.

Cook 1 to 1½ hours, depending on the thickness of the steaks and the cooking location.

Merritt Parkway Veal Scallopini

Winding its way through some of the most expensive residential real estate in the country, Connecticut's Merritt Parkway cries out for upscale recipes. This dish belongs on the engine of the newest, shiniest Volvo, or maybe a spiffy Saab turbo.

DISTANCE: 35–40 MILES

3/4 pound veal scallops
1/2 teaspoon tarragon
1 (4-ounce) jar roasted peppers, drained
Salt and pepper to taste

At home or on the road, place the slices of veal on the counter (or on the board you carry in your trunk) and pound thin with the heel of your hand (or see **Abalone Allanté,** page 118). Give the tarragon and peppers a whirl in the Cuisinart, or mince them finely with a knife. Place half of the veal scallops on individual pieces of buttered foil, spread with the puree, season with salt and pepper, and top with the remaining scallops. Wrap.

Cook about 40 minutes.

If you want to get fancy, you can roll the scallops with the puree jelly-roll style, 1 or 2 rolls to a package. The cooking time may be increased, but since the packages will be smaller, you'll have more options as to where to put them. Be careful that they don't drop out into the road—the Merritt, like many scenic routes, is full of sharp curves, and if someone's Pirellis fail to get purchase on a red-pepper slick and they career off into the trees, you'll be hearing from a very high-priced lawyer.

Veal Chop Forestiere

One of us, the one who lives at the end of a Vermont drive-way that would have daunted Scott of the Antarctic, finally went out and bought an all-wheel-drive Subaru. We had long been American-car loyalists—that is, ever since the '73 BMW we had bought new died in '82 and we found out what the damned things had come to cost—so this was a major life change. The shock was softened somewhat by the fact that this Subaru is called the Forester, which might be the first car name the Japanese have ever thought up that actually means something. (What the hell is a "Camry," or an "Impreza," or a "Sentra"?) In order to further salve our Eurocentric souls, we've teamed the doughty little green snow-buggy up with a French veal chop recipe, *forestiere* being a term describing any dish made with wild mushrooms.

Time to drive down to the mailbox. We'll be back when the veal is done. . . .

DISTANCE: 75 MILES

¹/₄ pound wild mushrooms (cèpes, chanterelles, morels, etc.), sliced
2 tablespoons veal stock (better yet, veal demiglace, if you've made any lately)
1 teaspoon cognac
2 tablespoons heavy cream
Salt and pepper to taste
1 loin veal chop, about 1 inch thick

At home, sauté the mushrooms briefly in butter. A couple of minutes before the mushrooms are done, add all the other ingredients except the veal. Turn up the heat and reduce the liquid by one-third.

Put a thin coating of the mushroom mixture on a sheet of foil. Lay the veal chop on top, and spread with the remainder of the mushroom mixture. Wrap carefully—this one contains more liquid than most—and then finish triple-wrapping. If you have room on the engine (and you should look for a hot spot for this one), repeat the whole thing and invite a friend along for the drive. The veal is done when still slightly pink inside.

Enzo's Veal

In honor of the late Enzo Ferrari.

DISTANCE: 75 MILES

1 pound veal scallops
$1/4$ cup minced sun-dried tomatoes
1 small red onion, finely minced
3 cloves garlic, minced
$1/4$ pound prosciutto, sliced paper-thin
1 teaspoon rosemary, crushed
Salt and pepper to taste

At home or on the road, place the slices of veal on the counter (or on the board you carry in your trunk) and pound thin with the heel of your hand (or see **Abalone Allanté,** page 118). Place half of the veal scallops on individual pieces of buttered foil. Add a layer of sun-dried tomatoes, onion, and garlic. Cover with a couple of strips of proscuitto, and sprinkle with the rosemary, salt, and pepper. Then top each with another veal scallop, and wrap tightly.

Start this in Manhattan and lunch will be ready in New Haven. Turn once, in Stamford. Total cooking time should be about 1 hour and 20 minutes.

Eggs in Purgatory

You don't have to cook these in purgatory, but if you feel the penitential urge, make them while going around and around the Tonnelle Avenue traffic circle in Jersey City. The recipe works best on cars with a large horizontal cooking surface that gets fairly hot, such as an injector housing that lies fairly close to the engines. It also involves the use of some auxiliary equipment, i.e., washed-out tuna or cat-food cans. These are handy items, by the way, to include in your road kitchen kit.

DISTANCE: 55 MILES

Spicy tomato sauce (either make your own or add
a good amount of red pepper flakes and/or hot
sauce to a commercial variety)
Eggs

At home or on the road, butter the insides of the cans well, and into each one place about 5 tablespoons of tomato sauce. Break one egg into each can, being careful not to break the yolk, then cover with roughly another 5 table-spoons of sauce.

Tightly wrap each can in foil so there will be no spilling, and set on your flat engine surface.

NOTE: Make sure you do the foil-cone test for hood clearance, as outlined on page 24, before you try this recipe. If the cone smashes down to a height exactly the same as the cans, you're in luck—the insulation pad under the hood will hold them in place for you. If the space is smaller than the cans, give up. Think what a damned fool you'll look like with tuna cans outlined in bas-relief on your hood. If the space is larger, use our foil-wad security system (see page 24). But put the foil wads *under* the cans, rather than over, because the cans will be soft on top.

If you can work out all these logistics, the cooking time on a hot engine should be about 1 hour. The idea is for the whites of the eggs to be set, with the yolks still runny. Uncover and poke the whites gently to check.

Eggs-On Cheese Pie

This recipe, which originated in a medieval monastery, has also been adapted to the tuna-can school of injector-housing cookery. If cholesterol were measured in octane, this would be right up there with leaded super.

DISTANCE: 55 MILES

Bread crumbs
1/2 pound mozzarella, diced
6 eggs
Salt and pepper to taste

At home or on the road, butter the insides of 6 washed tuna cans. (Scale the recipe down if you don't have room for 6 cans on your engine.) Toss a couple of tablespoons of bread crumbs into each can, shake to distribute, and dump out the excess. Cover the bottom of the cans with about half of the diced mozzarella, then break an egg into each can. Add salt and pepper, then cover with the remaining mozzarella.

Cover tightly, as per **Eggs in Purgatory** (page 69), and make sure you have good contact with the engine surface. Cook about 1 hour, until the cheese is melted and the eggs are set.

Pat's Provolone Porsche Potatoes

As opposed to the couch variety.

DISTANCE: 55 MILES

$^1/_2$ pound new potatoes
1 cup milk
1 cup water
2 ounces aged provolone, grated
Butter

At home, peel the potatoes and slice about $^1/_4$ inch thick. Place in a saucepan with the milk and water and simmer about 10 minutes. Drain and spread on heavily buttered foil—the number of packages you make is up to you, depending on the characteristics of your engine. We recommend at least 2, for optimum heat distribution. Sprinkle the potatoes with the grated provolone and dot with butter, then wrap.

Cook about 1 hour.

Speedy Spedini

This is a classic Italian recipe. Stick these small bread-and-cheese sandwiches onto the mill in your Ferrari, and you'll be looking forward to stopping rather than speeding.

DISTANCE: 40 MILES

1 (2-ounce) can anchovy fillets
$^1/_4$ cup chicken stock
1 loaf good-quality Italian bread,
   about 3 inches in diameter
$^3/_4$ pound mozzarella, preferably fresh

At home, drain the anchovies and mash with a fork. Add the chicken stock to make a thin paste. Slice the bread into $^1/_2$-inch rounds, and slice the cheese into $^1/_4$-inch slices. Make triple-decker sandwiches, using 3 slices of bread and 2 slices of cheese for each, and brushing the inside surfaces of the bread with the anchovy spread. Wrap each sandwich individually in buttered foil.

Cook until the cheese is runny, about 45 minutes.

Down-the-Shore Cavatelli, Sausage, and Broccoli Rabe

For a recent summer jaunt, we hopped in a convertible and headed down the Garden State Parkway to the Jersey Shore. It was our first trip down the shore (that's the proper expression) in maybe twenty-five years, and it did our hearts good to see that aside from the transformation of Atlantic City into Vegas East, the rest of the place has stayed pretty much the same—which is to say, there's an Italian restaurant on every block, and in places like Seaside Heights, there's a pizza stand for every ten boards on the boardwalk. The Jersey Shore is so imbued with the tradition of Italian eateries that proprietors change their names to sound Italian—we found a restaurant called Duffinetti's, started by a guy named Duffy, and a bagel shop (probably run by an Eddie Cohen) called Bageleddi's. There are sub shops down there that sell scungilli and big plates of escarole and beans. It's that Italian.

This recipe was inspired by a dish we enjoyed at a joint in Lavalette that was all pink inside, with big mirrors. Cook it while driving in a car to match.

DISTANCE: 70 MILES (POINT PLEASANT TO A.C.),
LESS IN HEAVY TRAFFIC (SOUTHBOUND ON FRIDAY NIGHT,
NORTHBOUND SUNDAY NIGHT)

2 cups cavatelli, cooked al dente
1/4 bunch broccoli rabe, coarsely chopped
2 links Italian sausage, hot or sweet, thinly sliced
3 tablespoons grated Parmesan
2 tablespoons olive oil
3 tablespoons dry white wine

1 to 2 cloves garlic, finely minced
Dash of red pepper flakes (optional)
Salt and pepper to taste

At home, toss all of the ingredients in a bowl. Heap onto foil and wrap. The dish is done when the sausage is no longer pink.

Thruway Thighs

This is a yupped-up version of that old New England tradition, poultry stuffed with oyster dressing. Cook it while driving to your condo in the "new Boston" or the "new Portland," or, if fate has so decreed, the "new Lawrence, Massachusetts," which looks just like the old one.

DISTANCE: 50–200 MILES,
DEPENDING ON CAR (SEE BELOW)

2 medium or 3 small leeks, white parts thinly sliced
1 fennel bulb, with stalks, thinly sliced
4 tablespoons butter
1/2 cup chicken broth
1 dozen oysters, shucked, the liquor retained (you can buy
    already-shucked fresh or frozen oysters in the fish section
    of your supermarket)
Salt and pepper to taste
8 chicken thighs, boned and butterflied

At home, gently sauté the leeks and fennel in 2 tablespoons of the butter, then braise in the chicken broth until soft. Drain, reserving the broth. Meanwhile, sauté the oysters in the remaining butter until their edges curl. Thoroughly combine the leeks, fennel, and oysters (break up the oysters, which will help you distribute them better), moistening with the reserved chicken broth or oyster liquor if necessary. Add salt and pepper.

Now lay the chicken thighs on individual pieces of buttered foil. Distribute the stuffing mixture among the thighs, folding one-half of each thigh over the other and sealing tightly.

This delicious dish nicely illustrates the variations in cooking times among different engines. The first time we tried it, on a trip up the Maine coast in a 1988 Chrysler New Yorker (that was the same day we cooked the game hens on the injector housing), it took 3 hours and 45 minutes to cook the thighs to perfection. Not that it wasn't worth the gas—food writer Alan Richman, who was along for the ride and the feed that day, granted us a "Hey, this stuff is really good!" and gave the recipe its charming alliterative name. But a couple of months later, in the hills near Santa Barbara, an '88 Olds Cutlass did the job in only 50 minutes. The big difference was that on the Chrysler, we placed the thighs in and around the fuel-injector ports. On the Cutlass, they went straight onto the exhaust manifold, which happened to be very accessible. Good thing we didn't have the Chrysler out there, because there wouldn't have been anyplace to stop for fried clams while the chicken was cooking.

Upper-Class Roadkill

Sometimes Madison Avenue takes a few too many hormone shots, and curious things happen. Take the ad copy for the new Lexus GS that came out around Halloween.

We thought that *Masters of the Universe* was a defunct Saturday morning kids' TV show, but apparently the concept is alive and well at whatever ad agency Lexus employs. What are we supposed to make of copy that reads "*A* is for the anxious deer afraid to cross the road / *B* is for the brazen growl 300 horses bode / *C* is for the chilling tune the conquering party hums / *D* is for the divining truth . . ." Well.

This scary bit of doggerel ends with the line "Something wicked this way comes." Then the ad segues into "Hell hath no fury like the seethings of a 300-horsepower . . ." blah blah blah. We wondered how on earth we were supposed to respond to these dark rhythms, when suddenly we realized: It all has to do with dinner.

Connecticut, with the highest income per capita in the country—not to mention a fair sprinkling of Lexus owners—is the perfect state for this recipe, thanks to a recent ruling that drivers who kill Bambi on the state's roads can keep the carcass if they wish. As Mr. Mies van der Rohe said, form follows function.

The first part of the recipe is a bit dicey: Mainly, take your brave vehicle out onto the Merritt Parkway and kill a deer, one that is anxious but not too afraid to cross the road. This shouldn't be too hard, though—on some mornings, that quaint highway looks like the local butcher's delivery-van door swung open and half the stock popped out. Stop and grab dinner. Once you've dressed and aged the meat, proceed as follows:

1 pound chanterelle mushrooms, sliced
2 shallots, minced
1¹/2 pounds aged venison flank, about 1 inch thick
1 tablespoon juniper berries (or, if you're in Connecticut, 2
   tablespoons of gin—it will evaporate in cooking, leaving
   the juniper flavor)
1 teaspoon rosemary, crushed
Salt and pepper to taste

At home, sauté the mushrooms and shallots in butter. Put
the venison on a sheet of foil, cover with the mushrooms
and shallots, and sprinkle with the seasonings. Wrap, place
on the engine, and start driving, humming a chilling tune.

Stuffed Whole Fish

This is quite a production and is probably suited only to a large engine, maybe an old in-line six with a hefty side manifold. Use any firm-fleshed, nonoily fish. A small striped bass or large red snapper would be ideal. The presentation is much nicer with the head on, but you can take it off if space dictates. Headroom in cars isn't what it used to be.

DISTANCE: 140 MILES

1 stick butter
3/4 pound fresh mushrooms, minced
1 pound fresh spinach
2 egg whites
Dash of nutmeg
Salt and pepper to taste
1 small red onion, finely minced
1 whole fish, 3 to 4 pounds

At home, first prepare the stuffing. Melt the butter in a saucepan, and when foaming, add the mushrooms. Stir and reduce the heat to a simmer. Cook, stirring frequently, until the liquid has evaporated and you're left with a creamy mass. Set aside. Rinse the spinach and remove the tough stems, then cook in a small amount of boiling water about 5 to 10 minutes. Drain, pressing out the excess water, then chop very fine. Beat the egg whites until frothy, and then blend with the spinach, adding the nutmeg, salt, pepper, and onion.

Place the fish on a cutting board. With a thin boning knife, cut along both sides of the backbone from the top to the bottom of the fish until the bone is free. Sever the backbone just behind the head and at the base of the tail, and lift it out, leaving the two sides of the fish joined at the head and tail.

Spread the spinach mixture between the fillets, topping with a layer of the mushroom mixture. Carefully wrap the fish in buttered foil, taking care to preserve its shape.

Cook about 2½ hours, turning once (*very carefully*). If you can pull this off, we'll let you contribute to the next edition of *Manifold Destiny*.

Safe-at-Any-Speed Stuffed Eggplant

Italians aren't the only ethnics in the Middle Atlantic region. Like Ralph Nader, this dish has a Middle Eastern pedigree. Like the Corvair, if you handle it right, you don't have to turn it over.

DISTANCE: 165–220 MILES

1 medium eggplant (about 1 pound)
3/4 pound ground lamb
1 medium onion, chopped
1 clove garlic, minced
1/2 teaspoon ground coriander
Salt and pepper to taste

At home, split the eggplant in half and scoop out the inside, leaving 1/2 inch of flesh on the hollowed shells. Dice the flesh you have scooped out, then set aside both the shells and the flesh. Lightly sauté the lamb in olive oil with the onion, garlic, and seasonings. Toss with the diced eggplant and sauté 5 minutes longer. Mound the mixture in both halves of the eggplant and wrap the halves individually in foil.

Place on the engine with skin side down. Plan a long trip; the cooking time will be 3 to 4 hours.

THE MIDWEST

The Midwest is where New England's solid Yankee fare took root on enormous prairie farms and in lunch-bucket industrial cities. Long hours spent in the fields or the foundry translate into prodigious appetites, which is how midwestern food got its reputation for density and heft. They don't serve "medallions" of anything out here, they serve manhole covers.

What's more, a funny thing happened to midwestern cookery on its way through the nineteenth century. It met up with the least subtle cuisine on earth, that of the Scandinavians and central Europeans, who came to make machine tools and tend dairy cattle. If you think chicken and dumplings is serious business, how about a couple of pig's knuckles?

Finally, the midwestern palate has come to reflect midwesterners' status as the national control group. Why do you think the phrase "Will it play in Peoria?" came about? We'll give you a hint: It wasn't because Peoria is the home of the American avant-garde. It's the same with food. Midwestern cooking is common-denominator cooking. The folks there not only want plenty of it on the plate, but also want it to be not too weird. Our big food conglomerates know this, which is why they test-market new flavors of instant pudding in Iowa rather than lower Manhattan.

For the car-engine cook, the Midwest is hallowed ground. Not only is the native cuisine admirably suited to a cooking method that is imprecise, forgiving, and innocent of fine nuances, but it comes from the very same part of the country that gave us the American car in all its classic glory. Short of reciting the pledge of allegiance with a mouthful of apple pie, what could be more patriotic than cruising around the heartland with something nice and filling bubbling away on the engine block of a Detroit leviathan—if not an old two-ton sedan, then maybe a mammoth sport-ute?

Last but not least, the Midwest is great driving country. No, not for harrowing downshifts on hairpin turns, but for cooking basic fare to the locally esteemed fare-thee-well while barreling down mind-numbing, 400-mile straightaways. It's a perfect marriage of cuisine and terrain.

Just remember, in the Midwest, *dinner* is what you cook in the morning and eat at noon. After an afternoon drive, it's *supper* you're taking off the engine.

Mom's Tuna Wiggle

Here's where we depart from the editorial "we" that has been making you think, erroneously, that we drive the same car, take the same trips, and eat the same food. "We" don't have the same mom, either. Although Maynard's mother was born and raised in Rhode Island, her culinary spirit is pure heartland, and the following was a standard offering when he was a kid. It's food like this that makes people become cooks.

This is a quintessentially American dish that should be cooked on the engine of a quintessentially American car. Now that the Chevy Caprice and Buick "Roadmonster" are gone, we suggest a Ford Crown Victoria or Mercury Grand Marquis, the latter of which has the accent on the "Grand Ma." No funny business here—just meat, potatoes, and a five-liter V-8. When the world has gotten so hip that there are only six Kiwanis members left, they'll hold their meetings in a Crown Vic. For this luncheon, we suggest Mom's Tuna Wiggle.

DISTANCE: 55–1,000 MILES

1 package frozen green peas
1 can light tuna in oil, drained and flaked

At home or on the road, thaw the peas enough so that they can be separated. In a mixing bowl—or in a clean hubcap—combine the peas and the tuna. Dump the glop on a sheet of foil and make a reasonably neat package.

Throw it on the engine and cook about 1 hour. The peas *should* be overdone.

NOTE: Since this makes a relatively soft package, it's ideal for molding around various odd shapes.

Dwight David Eisenhower
Pepper Steak

Note that we don't use the East Coast affectation *au poivre*. According to an old *Life* magazine, this was Ike's favorite food. It's a great recipe for cooking on the engine of some classic piece of 1950s Detroit iron.

DISTANCE: 55 MILES

¹/₄ cup whole peppercorns
1 small strip steak, ¹/₂ to ³/₄ pound

At home or on the road, crush the peppercorns with a mallet, rolling pin, tire iron, or jack handle, then spread them over both sides of the steak, pressing them in with your fingers to make them stick. Wrap in foil.

Cook about 30 minutes per side while driving through Kansas—longer if not directly on an engine hot spot, or shorter if you like 'em rare.

Hot Dog Surprise

The surprise is that people still cook these. We first encountered them back in Cub Scout days, when Ike was still chow-
ing down on pepper steak.

DISTANCE: 40 MILES

10 hot dogs
American cheese (or boutique-brand Wisconsin Cheddar, if
    you have an expensive car), sliced into hot dog–length
    fingers
10 slices bacon

At home or on the road, cut a deep slit in each wiener, and
stuff with fingers of cheese. Then wrap on the diagonal, like
an old bias-ply tire, with the bacon. Seal individually in foil.

These are great for stuffing into those odd places on the engine where you can't fit a turkey or a suckling pig. Cook
about 45 minutes or until the cheese is melted and the
bacon is somewhat crisp.

JB's Mall Pups

This is great for those lazy Saturdays when all you feel like doing is cruising the malls. Since all the ingredients are already cooked, you can just leave them on the manifold and dip in for a few after a grueling stint in the Liz Claiborne sale section.

DISTANCE: 25–30 MILES

2 (5-ounce) cans Vienna sausage
3 tablespoons cheap bourbon
1 teaspoon sugar

At home or on the road, neatly line up the sausages in a double row on a sheet of foil. Sprinkle with the bourbon and sugar. Seal neatly and add another layer of foil (we'll let you get away with just 2 layers on this one), pressing it tightly around the sausages so they'll brown.

They should be ready after half an hour on the engine, but are best eaten after the sugar caramelizes with the bourbon. Since car engines retain heat for a while after they're shut off, the sausages should stay warm for a long time—unless you run into a great sale.

Milwaukee Tube Steaks

No, not inner tubes. Drive west over the Milwaukee River heading away from the downtown financial district, turn left toward the old Schlitz brewery, and you'll find yourself at Usinger's, home of some of the best commercially produced sausages in the United States. They run the gamut from fresh bratwurst, smoked bratwurst, and baurenwurst to things like blutwurst, which tastes like it's made from bad dreams.

DISTANCE: 55–85 MILES

Sausage—your choice
Good mustard

At home or on the road, smear butter on foil and put down a selection of fresh sausages, as many as you think your hottest engine-cooking spot will accommodate. Spread a little mustard over them and wrap. It's important to wrap the foil tightly around the sausages if you want them to brown, and not to leave any stranded in the center of the package.

Cook 1 to 1½ hours, turning once. They should get you from Milwaukee to Sheboygan, where they have a distinctive style of bratwurst all their own.

Out-of-the-Fire, onto-the-Engine Stew

When we were lads, we both belonged to chapters of a uniformed organization devoted to woodcraft, knot-tying, and discipline. Looking back, we realize that the major purpose of this tent-raising and marching society was to keep boys occupied until they were old enough to drive. It's probably significant that the only conceivable activity they didn't award a badge for was driving.

We recently leafed through some of the recipes that got us through long, tedious, bug-bitten outings back in our paramilitary prepubescence, and came up with this number, ideally suited to motorized hiking. Put it on your block and see if anyone salutes.

DISTANCE: 85 MILES

1/4 pound meat (any kind), cut into 1/2-inch dice
3 vegetables you like (potatoes, carrots, onions, celeriac,
    etc.), cut into 1/2-inch dice
Salt and pepper to taste

At home or on the road, mix all of the ingredients and wrap in foil.

Originally, we cooked this on the coals of a roaring campfire; since we're all grown-ups now, put it on the engine and drive for 1 1/2 hours, turning at least once. (Don't blame us; it wasn't our idea to begin with.)

Candy-Apple-Red Chicken

Why would anyone combine sugar with canned tomato sauce and Worcestershire sauce? Don't ask. A good mid-western guest eats what's put on his plate.

DISTANCE: 85–110 MILES

1 chicken breast, split
$1/2$ cup chopped onion
$1/2$ cup chopped green pepper
$1/2$ teaspoon garlic powder
1 teaspoon oregano
1 (6-ounce) can tomato sauce
4 teaspoons brown sugar
1 tablespoon Worcestershire sauce
$1/4$ cup cider vinegar

At home, place each chicken breast half on a sheet of foil. Combine the remaining ingredients and ladle over the chicken. Wrap.

Cook $1^{1}/2$ to 2 hours.

Cruise-Control Pork Tenderloin

This is about as fancy as you dare get in the down-home Midwest, but it's okay if the pork tenderloin is from a native Iowa hog. The long cooking time will let you put a lot of prairie miles behind you. Just set the cruise control, line up your hood ornament with a distant landmark like the Nebraska state capitol, and set a timer to wake you up when dinner is ready.

DISTANCE: 250 MILES

3 tablespoons Dijon mustard
2 tablespoons dry white wine
1/2 cup red onion, minced
2 teaspoons rosemary, crushed
Salt and pepper to taste
1 pork tenderloin, 1 to 1 1/2 pounds, butterflied

At home or on the road, blend the mustard, wine, onion, and seasonings. Spread the split surface of the tenderloin with the mixture and press lightly together, then wrap with foil.

Find a medium-hot spot on the engine and turn once during cooking. Total cooking time should be about 4 1/2 hours.

Fupped Duck Catera

We had never really noticed that those birds on the Cadillac insignia were ducks—not until Caddy's brilliant ad agency came up with the $24 million idea of using a goofy cartoon duck to introduce the marque's new Euro-tourer model, the Catera. What's the deal here? Were there ducks on the coat of arms of Cadillac, the French explorer who penetrated deep into primeval Michigan?

We haven't driven the Catera, which looks to be a snappy little car, but we're more than a little concerned about whether Caddy is making the right move here. We know, we know . . . the idea is to snag a younger portion of the market, the Saab and Volvo and BMW crowd, instead of just hanging on to a demographic segment that will soon live entirely in Florida. But if we were GM's flagship division, we'd keep Caddies big and just sit back and wait, because the largest, richest, most talked-about-until-everybody-is-sick-of-them generation in history is within a decade's striking distance of the average Cadillac-buyer age of sixty-three. That's right—whether they know it or not, millions of fat-ass boomers are just waiting to slide into big, comfy De-Villes. And better yet, slide out of them without splitting their pants.

Aside from all that, there's the problem of the duck. We thought the duck was a dumb idea. So here he is, where he belongs, with a Cumberland sauce to match his red complexion.

2 slices duck breast, each about 3/4 inch thick
2 tablespoons red currant jelly
2 tablespoons port (ruby, not tawny)
1/2 teaspoon grated orange peel
1 teaspoon orange juice
Salt and pepper to taste

At home, make shallow diagonal cuts in both sides of the duck breast slices. Mix all of the other ingredients and simmer gently until slightly reduced. Spoon half of the mixture onto foil, place the duck breast slices on top, and top with the remaining sauce. Wrap carefully to contain the liquid. Find a reasonably hot spot and cook until the red juices are from the sauce, not the duck—but don't overcook, or the duck will be dry and tough, not at all like the cute duck in the Caddy commercials.

Any-City Chicken Wings

By now, "Buffalo" chicken wings have been consumed by millions who have no idea where Buffalo is, or that it is actually the threshold of the great Midwest. This is perfectly fine, since most of the bar cooks who make them don't know where it is either. This recipe is based on the premise that since you can call something anything you want, you can also put anything you want into it.

DISTANCE: 140–200 MILES

18 chicken wings
1/2 cup tomato catsup
1 cup red wine vinegar
4 to 6 canned jalapeño peppers, drained and minced (more
    if you like wings really hot)
3 cloves garlic, minced
1 tablespoon oregano
1 teaspoon red pepper flakes
Salt to taste

At home, place the chicken wings in a bowl. Blend the remaining ingredients in a second bowl, and then pour over the chicken wings. Cover tightly and refrigerate for 24 hours, stirring occasionally. Drain the wings, retaining the marinade liquid, and divide them among 3 sheets of foil. Brush with the remaining marinade.

Cook from Buffalo to Ashtabula, Ohio, if you know where either city is. Total cooking time will be about 2 1/2 hours. If they aren't done at Ashtabula, press on to Cleveland (another hour down I-90).

Lead-Foot Stuffed Cabbage

Stuffed cabbage is a dish that can be pleasingly filling or heavy as lead, depending on what goes into it. In this version, the food sociologist can observe the effects of several generations of simplifying Americanization on an old eastern European favorite. Pop a few of these down your throat while you're pounding down some godforsaken stretch of rust-belt interstate, and the accumulated weight will sink all the way to your right foot.

NOTE: These are best prepared in a ten-year-old Caprice with a YOU BETCHA DUPA I'M POLISH sticker on the rear bumper.

DISTANCE: 55 MILES

1 small green cabbage
1 pound ground beef
1 cup uncooked rice
2 cubes beef bouillon
2 cans condensed tomato soup
Salt and pepper to taste

At home, separate the leaves of the cabbage, discarding the tough outer ones and removing the inner ones intact. Drop into boiling water. After 10 minutes, drain and rinse with cold water.

Cook the beef in a skillet, breaking up with a spoon, until the pink color is gone. Do not drain the fat. Meanwhile, cook the rice in 2 cups of water along with the bouillon cubes until the water is absorbed and the rice is done. Combine the rice, meat, and 1 can of the soup (do not add water), and season with salt and pepper.

One by one, lay a blanched cabbage leaf flat, drop some stuffing on it, and roll up, forming a neat bundle with both ends sealed. Repeat until you run out of cabbage or stuffing.

Place the rolls on foil in pairs, smearing each with a generous amount of soup from the second can. Wrap.

Find a good place for them on the engine and drive about 1 hour, depending on the size of your cabbage leaves.

To Grandmother's House Road Turkey

Unless you haul the family around at holiday time in a Greyhound bus, you'd be pretty hard-pressed to engine-roast a whole turkey on the way to the in-laws. These individual portions will not only solve the space problem; when they're done, they'll keep the kids amused in the backseat. Afterward, cleaning up the mess can be made into a family game, with extra cookies for the one who finds the most shards of tinfoil in the upholstery. (Keep the used foil away from the dog if you want to have a happy holiday.)

DISTANCE: 220 MILES

1 boneless turkey breast, about 5 pounds, sliced into thin
    strips against the grain
3 large baking potatoes, peeled and diced
3 carrots, finely diced
Dry white wine
Flour for dredging
Salt and pepper to taste
3/4 cup heavy cream

At home, combine the turkey, potatoes, and carrots in a bowl with wine to cover. Marinate for 2 hours in the refrigerator, then drain well (*don't* drink the wine). Setting the vegetables aside, dredge the turkey pieces in flour, then heavily butter 5 large squares of foil. Arrange equal amounts of turkey and vegetables on each square, and season with salt and pepper as desired. Cup the foil around the turkey and vegetables, and pour over each serving as much heavy cream as you can without making a soupy mess, then seal carefully.

Cook on the engine about 4 hours, turning once. We're assuming that Grandma doesn't live in the next town.

Curmudgeon's Capered Lamb

We'd like to end this section, which has been dedicated to traditional American values in food and cars, with a gratuitous gripe against bizarre additions to automobiles in the name of progress. We're thinking in particular of those new display screens that show a street map of your preferred city, with the best route to your punched-in destination lit up. This disturbs us on two counts. First, it is a direct refutation of the time-honored tradition of misleading or missing signage. As practiced in the approaches to Chicago, for instance, this gives a hapless driver the distinct impression that if he doesn't know where he is, he shouldn't be driving there. Given false confidence by the dashboard video maps, how many poor souls are going to be smashed into oblivion as they try to read a computer screen purporting to show the intersection of the Dan Ryan, Adlai Stevenson, and JFK expressways as they careen toward the Loop?

The other problem we have with this trend is that once it's been around for a few years, you'll be laughed off the road for being totally unhip if you don't have one of the damned things. (Why do you suppose there's an outfit in California making fake car phones?) The whole situation is not unlike the embarrassment you'd suffer in one of Manhattan's wear-all-black-and-make-sure-it's-too-big-for-you restaurants if you ordered lamb medium-well, and please hold the lingonberry and kimchi sauce. Women wouldn't look at you after that faux pas, even if you were wearing *two* Rolexes.

Lamb is like cars, and not only because they make a lot of both out in Middle America. Lamb gives you the opportunity to state your retro preferences, as in this midwestern recipe.

4 lamb chops
$1/2$ cup capers, drained and finely chopped
Juice of 1 lemon
Salt and pepper to taste

At home or on the road, sprinkle both sides of the chops with the capers, lemon juice, salt, and pepper. Wrap snugly.

Cook about 1 hour, turning once. (This works best if you can get the chops flat against the exhaust manifold.) If you like them fashionably pink—if, say, you are driving east— cook for a shorter time.

Practically overnight, it became fashionable to cook southern. Two distinct phenomena are responsible for America's sudden infatuation with Dixie at table. On the one hand, northern gastronomes finally realized that we have a native French cuisine within our borders after all, even if we did fail to capture Quebec during the Revolution. True, the culinary repertoire of Evangeline's Cajun descendants has crossbred with local influences that would make Montreal's eyes bug out, never mind Paris's, but the result is a distinct cuisine that can be mighty tasty, even though done to death by local premix entrepreneurs and by gimmick-happy Yankee chefs who would blacken a doorstop if they thought somebody would buy it and eat it.

The other culinary trend that has turned America's attention southward is the craze for "comfort food." Lord knows all food should be comforting, but when we started treating ourselves like finely tuned machines that run on oat bran and yogurt, we somehow forgot that basic truth (we the society, not we the shameless omnivores who wrote this book). So now the pendulum swings back the other way, and we turn to the South for solace—i.e., calories.

The pickup truck is the obvious instrument of choice for cooking southern food, though a case could be made for a sedan with heavy-duty springs if you want to become a serious disciple of Paul Prudhomme. A Cajun comfort car, you might call it. As for the proper combination of culinary and driving styles, well, if you go screaming through some one-horse town late at night in a car with out-of-state plates, just be sure you're cooking something down-home. Imagine some beady-eyed

Faulknerian cop asking you, "What's that smell, boy?" and then having to tell him that if he doesn't hurry up and write your ticket, the oysters in your Thruway Thighs are going to get overcooked.

Better you should be frying possum on that engine, boy.

Good and Simple
Cajun Shrimp/Crayfish

Driving down a highway like old U.S. 90, which goes east-west through Louisiana, you'll see lots of trucks in parking lots selling shrimp, crabs, and, if the season's right, crayfish. Stop and buy some, then go to the nearest vegetable stand and get some garlic, onions, and small green hot peppers. Now get cooking.

DISTANCE: 35 MILES

6 small green hot peppers
1 medium onion
2 cloves garlic
1 pound shrimp or crayfish tails, in their shells (if using
    shrimp, remove legs)

At home or on the road, remove the seeds from the peppers (a good reason to keep rubber gloves in your car), and mince finely, along with the onion and garlic. Spread the shrimp or crayfish on heavily buttered foil and cover with the vegetables. Wrap.

Cook about 40 minutes, until the shellfish are nice and pink. Cooking them in their shells adds flavor and gives you something to lick afterward.

"Cajun" Shrimp

Once while driving through Louisiana, we stopped to check out the shelves in a Pick and Pay supermarket in Lake Arthur. It was the first time we ever saw *gallon* jars of rendered pork fat in a butcher case. Next we browsed through the condiment and spice selections, and realized that a lot of what's been sweeping the country as "Cajun" cooking increasingly comes out of jars—jars of precooked roux, jars of spice mixes for meat and fish, jars with drawings of fat men on them. In short, what started out as a bona fide regional cuisine has become a premixed abomination designed to make fat people fatter. We don't know what the life expectancy is down there, but we do know that it's possible to travel through Cajun country for a week without encountering any food that isn't fried, with the exception of coffee and salad. Here's a sample, with the brand names deleted.

DISTANCE: 55 MILES

Rendered pork fat
1 pound of shrimp from the supermarket
Assorted jars of whatever "Cajun" seasonings you've seen
  advertised

At home or on the road, heat the fat until it liquefies. If you're a real die-hard car cook, you might want to do this on an idling engine, using one of the cleaned-out tuna cans you keep on hand to make **Eggs in Purgatory** (page 69) in the Northeast. Peel the shrimp and devein if they're large. Then dredge the shrimp in the fat and dust heavily with the powdered spices. Wrap in foil.

Place on a medium-hot part of the engine, and cook about 1 hour. It doesn't matter if the shrimp are overcooked, since you're eating a concept, not a food.

Blackened Roadfish

As in the previous recipe, think of the concept and not the food. What's important about this dish is driving along thinking, "I'm cooking blackened fish and you're not." It's the same idea as having a car that can go 150 mph even if you never get it over 65.

DISTANCE: 50 MILES

1 pound firm white fish fillets, cut thin
Your choice of premixed "Cajun" spices

At home or on the road, cover the fish on both sides with a heavy layer of spices, pressing them in with your hands. Place on foil spread with butter and wrap tightly.

Cook about 25 minutes per side.

NOTE: Some cars are decidedly better for this type of cooking than others. Take a cue from Cajun chefs, who heat their cast-iron skillets practically to the melting point, and go for an engine that has a maximum amount of exposed hot metal.

Orange Roughy Floribbean

Charles Darwin had to sign on to the *Beagle* for a no-frills world cruise in order to come up with the theory of natural selection. But we've got it easy: For incontrovertible proof that evolution is still humming along, all we have to do is go to the fish department in the supermarket. How else to explain entire new species of fish? For instance, who the hell ever heard of tilapia until a few years ago? We would have thought it was some crummy little town in a Faulkner novel—but, no, it's apparently an entirely new piscatorial development.

Same with orange roughy, the star of this recipe. When we first heard it mentioned, we were sure the reference was to a Protestant hoodlum in Belfast. Turns out it's a mild, firm-fleshed fish that fillets nicely and sells for about five bucks a pound (evolution now involves pricing along with all the biological details). It's amazing: We've looked and looked through *My First Book of Fishes,* the standard reference work we've used for years, and there's nary an orange roughy to be found.

Anyway, this new member of the fish club turns out to be perfectly suited for the "Floribbean" treatment, that Miami-based trend that involves tossing together fresh local fish, tropical produce, and, in many cases, sugar's leap at immortality. It's a South Beach kind of cookery, complete with an Art Deco color scheme. Cook this one on a flashy convertible—a white Chrysler Sebring, say, that won't clash with the pastel hotel facades on Ocean Drive.

Juice of 1 lime

$1/2$ jalapeño or $1/4$ Scotch bonnet pepper, minced (use rubber gloves)

2 orange roughy fillets, about $1/2$ pound total

1 yellow banana pepper, cut into thin strips

2 tablespoons dark rum

At home, squeeze the lime juice into a shallow bowl big enough to marinate the fish. Add the minced hot pepper, then place the fish in the lime-pepper marinade and turn. Marinate the fish for 30 minutes, turning once.

Lightly butter foil, and lay down half of the banana pepper strips. Splash 1 tablespoon of the rum on the peppers. Remove the fish from the marinade, taking along as much of the hot pepper bits as you care to, and place the fish atop the peppers. Arrange the remainder of the banana peppers over the fish, and splash with the remainder of the rum. Wrap securely, then add the remaining 2 layers of foil. Wedge into a hot spot and turn once during cooking.

NOTE: Divide the ingredients and prepare in 2 packets if the engine requires.

New Orleans Doves

What to do after an afternoon of dove hunting? An evening of dove eating.

DISTANCE: 40 MILES

4 tablespoons butter
1 cup vinegar
1 teaspoon red pepper flakes
1 tablespoon minced garlic
4 cleaned doves (2 per person)

At home, melt the butter and combine with the vinegar, red pepper flakes, and garlic. Baste the birds heavily, then wrap 1 or 2 to a package, depending on the space you have to accommodate them.

Cook about 45 minutes. (Start by placing the birds on the engine so that the breasts are firmly against a hot surface, and turn halfway through cooking.)

U.S. 17 Carolina Stuffed Crabs

This solves the problem of live ones scurrying off the engine block.

DISTANCE: 40–55 MILES

6 large blue crabs
5 tablespoons butter
15 sprigs fresh parsley, chopped
3 scallions, chopped
2 cups stale bread crumbs
Juice of 1 lemon

At home, boil the crabs. Pick through the meat and remove the cartilage, reserving the shells. Melt 2 tablespoons of the butter in a saucepan and sauté the parsley and scallions until limp. Add the crabmeat and heat briefly. Then, add the bread crumbs, lemon juice, and enough cold water to make a moist, firm stuffing. Fill the crab shells, dot with the remaining butter, and wrap.

Bake in medium-hot engine crannies 45 minutes to 1 hour.

Pickup Ham Steak

A lot of southern cooking, especially in the "comfort" category, seems to include staples like margarine and cheese. We're not saying it's good, but it's there. Enjoy it the way you might enjoy the decaying industrial landscape around Mobile or Memphis.

DISTANCE: 85 MILES

1 ham steak
Margarine
1 cup canned tomatoes, drained
$1/4$ pound unsliced American cheese, grated
1 small onion, minced
1 bay leaf
2 tablespoons minced fresh parsley
Pepper to taste
$1/4$ teaspoon thyme

At home, place the ham steak on margarined foil. Combine all of the other ingredients, spread over the ham, and seal tightly.

This can be a messy one. When you size up the cooking spots your engine affords, go for security rather than maximum heat. Don't worry about finding the manifold (the 45-degree slant of an '81 Toyota manifold has been known to cause a highway ham spill); this one is a natural for foil-wedging on top of the injector housing, or nestling in along the inside of a valve cover on an old V-8. Cook about $1\frac{1}{2}$ hours; if it needs more time, leave the engine running while you stop in at a roadhouse for a Jim Beam and Co'Cola.

Maryland Crab Imperial

A couple of years ago, we had to do a story that involved visiting every accessible lighthouse on the Chesapeake Bay. The assignment turned into a 1,000-mile *tour de crabe,* as we hit one joint after another that specialized in the bay's most famous denizens. Not counting soft-shells, which are a seasonal item relating to the creatures' molting schedule, we found that the vast majority of Chesapeake crabs tend to find their way onto the plate in one of three ways: boiled and served on a big sheet of brown paper with a mallet and pick, fried with batter as crab cakes or fritters, and—generally in places that have cloth napkins—in the casserole known as crab imperial.

As long as the basic recipe is sound, this last dish is a nice way to eat crabs. The brown-paper-mallet-and-pick approach is not only messy, but guilt-inducing: When you survey the pile of debris left after a hearty feed, you feel as if you've single-handedly put the crustaceans on the endangered species list. As for crab cakes and fritters, you're at the mercy of those cooks who hold up a crab so it can breathe on a big blob of batter, which is then fried without further crab involvement. But you can't really fake crab imperial, and you don't have to think about how many crabs actually went into a decent portion.

We have no idea where this dish got its imperialist name. But maybe you should cook it on an old Chrysler Imperial.

DISTANCE: 50 MILES

1 pound blue crab meat, picked over
$^1/_2$ green bell pepper, diced
1 pimiento, diced

Pinch of salt
A few gratings of white pepper
1 teaspoon dry mustard (mild, not Chinese hot)
2 tablespoons heavy cream
1 tablespoon dry sherry
1 egg, lightly beaten

At home or on the road, mix all of the ingredients, being careful not to break the crabmeat into tiny shreds.

Butter a sheet of foil. Mound the crab mixture on the foil and wrap carefully—make sure the final 2 wraps are tight enough to hold this fairly loose mixture, but leave enough room to mold the package on an appropriate engine surface (preferably one of the hotter ones). The dish is done when the egg has set.

CALIFORNIA AND POINTS WEST

One morning while we were stuck in traffic on I-680 outside San Jose, cursing the fact that our failure to get past the Bay Area before rush hour was going to cost us 600 points in the One Lap of America rally, we noticed that we were idling next to a business-suited woman in a BMW 325 with a crystal hanging from her rearview mirror. Not a graduation tassel, like in New Jersey, or a pair of fuzzy dice, like in east L.A., but a genuine crystal, possessed of God-knows-what secret powers—excluding, of course, the power to get a BMW out of Silicon Valley traffic jams. Right then and there it occurred to us that here was the very spirit of modern California, the perfect combination of mammon and mystery, the Bavarian and the Aquarian.

That becrystaled Bimmer was emblematic of the California approach to food as well. The idea is to take expensive, high-quality ingredients, and combine them in such a way as to make people burble over how imaginative and creative you are. We're talking about things like venison steak with smoked kidney and fruit brandy, or swordfish smeared with pounded duck livers. (Honestly, we didn't make these up.) It also helps if there isn't enough to eat—if fasting raises your consciousness, maybe half-fasting will raise it at least partway. This half-fast concept could only have come from California.

Actually, we're not sure if what has become known as California Cuisine exists outside of the state's restaurants. Californians may not cook this way at home—but then again, they may not cook or eat at home at all. We know people in L.A. who are proud of the fact that they don't even own forks, let alone pots and pans; they just eat out all the time. But since they spend a good part of each day in their cars, engine cooking may be just what they need to get back in the habit of preparing meals for themselves, all the while saving money that would be better spent on a place in Montana. To ease them back into cooking, we offer them a taste of the familiar. The rest of you can figure out how to substitute two pounds of sausage meat for the cilantro.

Poached Fish Pontiac

Pontiac is a many-splendored marque, several models of which fit in beautifully with the southern California scene. For Malibu, we recommend a mint 1956 Safari wagon, preferably in white. For cruising Mulholland Drive at sunset, you can't go wrong with a 1967 GTO, in any color but that awful army green they came out with. And over in the San Fernando Valley, it's got to be a late-model Trans-Am. Any one of them will cook this namesake fish dish to a turn.

DISTANCE: 40 MILES

1 thick fillet of firm white fish native to Pacific waters or
   1 halibut steak, about 3/4 pound
3 to 4 tablespoons dry vermouth or white wine
3 teaspoons minced shallots
1 bay leaf
White pepper to taste
Butter

At home or on the road, lay out a sheet of foil and butter it lightly. Place the fish on the foil, then tuck up the sides of the foil and sprinkle the vermouth or wine over the fish. Spread the shallots on top, then add the bay leaf, pepper, and a few dabs of butter. Close the foil carefully and wrap tightly.

Cooking time is approximately 45 minutes; check after 30 minutes if the fish is in direct contact with the manifold. The halibut steak will take longer than the fillet.

Three-Pepper Salmon Steaks

This is the perfect recipe to fix while dashing down Route 1 along the California coast in your BMW. Keep an eye on your crystal; waves of energy will emanate from it when the salmon is done. If you want to be super trendy, place a foil package of romaine lettuce on your engine about fifteen minutes before you and your crystal *think* the fish will be done. Next thing you know, you'll be serving salmon on wilted lettuce. To go with this dish, we recommend a nice bottled water, preferably a hard-to-find import.

DISTANCE: 55 MILES

1 tablespoon each black, pink, and green peppercorns,
    coarsely crushed (get out that tire iron)
3 salmon steaks, each about 1 inch thick (1 steak per
    person)
Olive oil (extra virgin, natch)

At home or on the road, press the pepper into both sides of the salmon steaks. Brush with oil and wrap.

Cook about 1 hour, turning when halfway done.

Open Sesame Fillet (Sesame Sole Food)

One of the most fiercely ubiquitous ingredients of the nineties has been any variation of sesame (*Sesamum indicum*). We think the trend grew out of the popularity of cold sesame noodles as a Chinese take-out item, probably because it doesn't matter if the delivery boy is slow—the stuff is cold anyway.

Many of today's chefs pay lip service to the idea of "fusion" cooking by adding a whack of either sesame oil or seeds to almost anything. Besides covering breadsticks, we've seen the seeds in guacamole, mixed with sprouts, and sprinkled over mesclun salads. In an Irish restaurant we frequent, one of the big hitters is a Caesar salad topped with strips of grilled sesame chicken. If you're out of seeds, you can always make do by frying or dressing whatever trendy foods you're eating with sesame oil.

Being purists, we prefer simplicity. This dish cooks best on a quiet, thoughtful car.

DISTANCE: 50 MILES

1 pound sole fillets
3/4 cup sesame oil
One bunch small scallions, including half of the green parts, thinly sliced
1/4 cup sake
Salt and pepper (freshly ground green or pink peppercorns would be ideal) to taste

At home, put the sole in a shallow bowl with the sesame oil and let stand about 1 hour, turning carefully several times. Drain the sole and divide into 4 portions on the foil. Sprinkle with the scallions, sake, salt, and pepper. Wrap. Place on engine and drive about one hour.

Abalone Allanté

Abalone is very hard to find, unless you are a member of one of California's protected colonies of sea otters. The only reason we're including a recipe here is so we can tell you how to tenderize it: Put the abalone flesh between clean pieces of 1/2-inch-thick plywood and drive back and forth over it a few times.

DISTANCE: 25–30 MILES

Fresh abalone, as much as your engine can accommodate
Lemon juice
Salt and pepper to taste

At home or on the road, place the tenderized pieces of abalone on well-buttered foil, and sprinkle with lemon juice, salt, and pepper. Wrap.

Cook about 30 minutes on or near the exhaust manifold. While you drive, listen to Albinoni's *Adagio* on the tape deck. Now say, "Abalone Allanté Albinoni's *Adagio*" five times fast.

Baked Gilroy Garlic Highway 101

Gilroy, California, as the signs will tell you as you approach town on Route 101, is the garlic capital of America. This is a good dish to cook while on your way to a date that will probably fizzle anyway. The primary purpose of the bread crumbs, by the way, is to act as a reservoir of oil for the cooking process.

DISTANCE: 55 MILES

3 heads garlic (if you can find it, the so-called elephant
    garlic is spectacular for this dish)
$^1/_2$ cup coarse bread crumbs
California olive oil, preferably from a small grove that
    numbers its pressings and buys its bottle graphics from
    artists waiting to get their first wine-label contracts

At home, separate the cloves of garlic, but do not peel. Place the garlic and bread crumbs in separate bowls and cover with oil, soaking them for 1 hour. Drain, then package about 10 cloves to a serving, sprinkling well with the bread crumbs. (You can recycle the oil for salad dressing.)

Place anywhere on the engine where there is a reasonable amount of heat, and cook until the garlic is very soft. You may be able to determine this without opening the packages. It should take about 1 hour.

Melrose Avenue Chicken

We named this dish after the avenue that was the heart of hip in Los Angeles nine years ago. It doesn't seem like much of a big deal anymore, although the "Melrose" cachet survives in secondhand fashion thanks to a cheesy TV show.

DISTANCE: 55 MILES

2 chicken breasts, boned and butterflied (1 breast per
    person)
1 green bell pepper
1 red bell pepper
2 yellow bell peppers (these cost the most, so it's important
    to use more of them)
1/4 cup California olive oil (see preceding recipe)
Cilantro
Salt and white pepper to taste

At home, pound each breast with the heel of your hand until thin. Slice the peppers thinly and sauté lightly in the oil. Lay an assortment of peppers on each breast, add a few snips of cilantro, and season with salt and pepper. Flop each breast over in half to form a neat package, and wrap separately.

Cook on the engine 1 hour, turning when halfway done.

Donner Pass Red-Flannel Hash

Say you're hanging out at your country place in the hills of Nixon, Nevada, and feel like having a soda. It's the weekend and a couple of friends from the East are visiting, so why not give them a taste of the countryside and head to Soda Springs, over the line in California? Take 447 down to I-80 and head west into the Sierra Nevada. Maybe you should take your new Chevy Tahoe, since Soda Springs is only about twenty-five miles northwest of that mile-and-more-high lake. But before you go, you might want to think about lunch.

For between you and Soda Springs is the 7,000-foot Donner Pass. With the sturdy Tahoe, you'll be tempted to take the back road, old Route 40, also known as the Donner Pass Road—what are four-wheel drives for, after all? While I-80 gets closed for only about five days each winter, Route 40 shuts down "every day there's a snowstorm," according to the California Highway Patrol unit at Truckee.

Keep the gas tank topped off, and bring some blankets—you never know how long you'll have to keep warm, waiting for the search party. And have provisions on hand, or you might be forced to make a rather large philosophical decision. We all know what happened at Donner Pass. How well do you want to know your friends?

The nice thing about hash is that you can make it with just about any kind of meat that's available. Also, we figure that in winter, a red flannel shirt is a standard part of the layered look, so we included beets. If you haven't brought them along, just toss in a piece of the shirt for color.

1 pound meat (beef, turkey, chicken, corned beef, or
   whatever is available), cubed
1 pound potatoes (or whatever wild root vegetables might
   be within arm's reach of the car), cubed
1 large onion (or maybe some wild ramps from under the
   snow), chopped
3 medium beets, boiled in their skins, then peeled and
   cubed
Chicken stock (or melted snow) to moisten
Salt and pepper to taste (or mask it)

At home or on the road, mix all of the ingredients well and
form into patties. Triple-wrap in foil, place on the engine,
and hope for company.

Corvette Stingray

Skate, or ray, is a much-neglected food, probably because people have seen too many underwater horror films. A big advantage is that since it is neglected, it is usually cheap if you can find it. Since you will not find it frozen in a Kroger's in the Midwest, it passes muster as a trendy California food.

DISTANCE: 55–85 MILES

1 stick butter
1 small red onion, chopped
$^1/_4$ cup capers, drained and minced
1 skate wing, cut into serving pieces

At home, melt the butter in a saucepan, add the onion and capers, and simmer over very low heat about 15 minutes. Place the pieces of skate on buttered foil, brush well with the onion-caper mixture, and wrap.

Cook 1 to 1$^1/_2$ hours on a medium-hot part of the engine, perhaps atop the injector housing. Be sure not to overcook, or you'll wind up with skate*board,* another California favorite.

Chicken Breast Lido

We named this dish after everyone's favorite auto corporation CEO, who, now that he's retired, owns olive groves in Tuscany and markets olive-oil products. If you can't find his brand, which is rated SAE 5W-30 for use in Chryslers, you can fall back on one of the better California oils.

DISTANCE: 140 MILES

2 ounces prosciutto, diced
1/2 cup shredded provolone
3 scallions, minced
1 chicken breast, boned and butterflied
Salt and pepper to taste

At home, mix together the prosciutto, provolone, and scallions. Place half of the chicken breast smooth side down, then spread the prosciutto mixture over it. Season with salt and pepper. Fold the other half of the breast over and press together gently. Place on foil that has been brushed with olive oil. Wrap.

Turn once during cooking. Cooking time, on a medium-hot spot, should be about 2 1/2 hours, less if you have access to the manifold.

It's a Wrap

Today's multi- (or omni-, for that matter) ethnic food sensation is the wrap. Obviously derived from the burrito, this handful of almost anything pouched in a flour tortilla bears the same relationship to real food as does a salad pizza or a sun-dried tomato bagel. It sort of looks like a duck, but the quack is funny and the gait is off.

In for a dime, in for a dollar. We've transplanted the wrap to Hawaii, fitting because the first thing many tourists do when they get there is wrap leis around their necks. Then, after a few too many pops at the luau, they get carried away and wrap grass skirts around their hips.

On our first trip to the islands, we never made if off Oahu, a great place to drive for the directionally impaired. If you start off in Honolulu and get lost, keep driving and sooner or later you'll wind up back on Waikiki, just in time for a lunchtime wrap on the beach.

DISTANCE: ABOUT 50 MILES, DEPENDING ON
HOW MANY BEACHES YOU STOP AT

For each wrap:
Peanut oil
1 (10-inch) flour tortilla
3 ounces roast pork, julienned
1/4 cup shredded fresh pineapple
3 tablespoons shredded coconut

At home or on the road, spread the peanut oil over a rectangle in the center of the tortilla, keeping in mind the shape of the final wrap.

Layer the remaining ingredients over the peanut oil. Wrap by folding up the bottom half of the tortilla, making a half circle, then folding the left and right sides over the center to make a presentable package. Using foil, wrap the wrap, and keep it on the engine long enough for it to heat through.

CAR-ENGINE RECIPES:
INTERNATIONAL CAR CUISINE

*G*lobal has been the watchword of the nineties—from the "New World Order" right down to this "global economy" we keep hearing about. (Near as we can figure, having a global economy means that if you get laid off from your job at the rolling mill in Kenosha, it's actually good for you, because, hey, it's a global economy.)

As the world goes, so goes *Manifold Destiny*. Far be it from us to get tagged as isolationists.

Nifty NAFTA Nachos

We would never think to question the fine, altruistic goals behind NAFTA—the North American Free Trade Agreement. To allow a brief moment of cynicism, though, the main beneficiaries seem to be outfits such as auto and apparel manufacturers that now get to use labor that is, to be polite, a tad less expensive than the going rate in the United States. We really haven't seen any stories about Canadian companies opening knit-hat plants in Bismarck, North Dakota, or Mexican entrepreneurs scouting factory space in Flint, Michigan, for their new widget assembly lines.

But enough of our silly caviling. In the spirit of free trade and international cooperation, we offer this treat.

Say you're parked, idling, on some dirt road just across the border from Chihuahua, where they grow the little dogs, in the Sierra Vieja Mountains, about twenty miles north of where Texas Route 170 comes to a dead end at Candelaria. You're waiting for your own private free trade shipment, which might take the form of either warm bodies or something to make the body warmer. Given the vagaries of your international partners' schedule for crossing the Rio Grande, you might get a bit peckish. Here's the answer: toasty nachos.

The best part of this recipe is that you can avoid commercial chips and use freshly made tortillas, thus gainfully employing the local populace.

Lard

4 (8-inch) corn tortillas

1 small can jalapeño peppers, thinly sliced

$1/2$ pound Monterey Jack cheese, or a good Cheddar,
   shredded

At home or on the road, grease 4 squares of foil with lard.
With a sharp knife, score, but do not cut through, each tortilla. Place 1 tortilla on each foil square, then distribute the
sliced peppers over all. Sprinkle with the cheese, and wrap
tightly. Place on the hottest available spot on the engine and
cook until crisp, 30 to 45 minutes. Unwrap, crack at the
score marks, and chow down.

Depending on the size of your manifold and the length of
your wait, we suggest cooking each batch in succession, to
pass the time and ensure freshness. Watch your back.

Bento Boxster

Recently, we took a look at the Boxster, Porsche's newest roadster and its first production model with a flat six. It's a lovely little chunk of Teutonic steel (and aluminum and titanium and a lot of other materials not found in the old Spyder), with a sensuality missing from BMW's shoe box Z-3. The only thing we didn't see was the engine.

And you can't, either. The Boxster's 2.5 liter, twenty-four-valve mill may crank out 201 horsepower, but it's not going to produce those horses while you're watching. In the ultimate display (or nondisplay) of car coyness, the engine is accessible only from the bottom of the car. Lift the hood and you'll see cargo space. Lift the trunk lid and you'll see the same. The Boxster makes nice noises, but you can't see where they're coming from.

In a way, this seems like an odd marketing miscalculation, depriving the American male car-owner of the time-honored tradition of standing in front of an open hood, dreamily gazing at his new engine, watching the shiny clockworks jiggle nicely as the exhaust burbles away. Poke the throttle linkage and hear it go *vrooom*. Man and boy are once more interchangeable.

As far as the subject in front of us, lunch, goes, it's a disaster. Obviously, we're not going to suggest that you lie on your back and blindly pack Kassler Rippchen up into any spot that will hold it, or maybe cram a couple of pounds of spaetzle into some mysterious cavity. But being bright boys, we found the solution.

1 bento box of sushi per occupant, purchased from your
   favorite sushi joint (if you own a Boxster, you'll have a
   favorite sushi joint)

On a cool to cold day, put the bento box(es) into the front
or rear trunk and drive like hell to someplace else.

Stop the car, retrieve the sushi, and eat it.

Don't try to eat while you're driving, lest you spill soy sauce
on whichever of the six optional leather surfaces you've se-
lected for the seats. While desperately trying to clean the
leather, you'll probably flip the thing, winding up with a
bent Boxster and no lunch.

MRE Leg of Lamb

With little access to the action during the Persian Gulf War, some of the news media passed their time fixating on odd tangents. Television people like to have something they can actually show the audience, and one popular Gulf War item was the MRE (meal, ready to eat), the descendant of the C and K rations of earlier conflicts. The other big (over three tons) media darling was the Humvee.

This giant all-terrain vehicle, looking like the world's biggest jeep with camouflage paint (light brown for the desert) and inverted *V*s on its flanks, became—in its civilian version—America's must-have set of wheels for the macho-and-mucho-bucks set. Even more than the Lincoln Navigator and Ford Expedition—and the soon-to-appear Cadillac sport-ute—the Humvee represents the extreme, over-the-top end of 4WD madness. The Ford and Lincoln can at least be understood in terms of man's eternal desire to own a seven-passenger Pierce-Arrow touring sedan. The Humvee, however, can be explained only in terms of an atavistic urge to crush the Carthaginians.

We lived for a mercifully brief period in Venice (the one off the Santa Monica Freeway, not the one of San Marco and the Gritti palace), and parked our car in a garage across from Arnold Schwarzenegger's restaurant. Being a big, muscular guy, he was one of the early purchasers of this big, muscular vehicle. The odd thing was, it was always parked with an entire space on either side. We never figured out whether this was to guard against dings or because he just couldn't park something that big.

Anyway, for all those guys who missed WW II (the big one), we've combined these two big media hits of the brief Gulf War, which, as we go to press, we hope won't wind up being called GW I. Try this recipe as you cruise across the desert (Iraqi or Mojave, depending on how things are going).

Or, on the more prosaic side, you might be like the self-described baby boomer in a recent news story who uses her Hummer, the civilian version of the Humvee, to commute twenty miles to work in the Midwest. Realizing that she's an absentminded driver, she got the thing for protection, apparently unconcerned about how many other drivers might qualify for Purple Hearts as she barrels down the road. Having one of these beasts because you're dangerous to the motoring world seems like giving a little .22 plinker to the average wacky teenager, while awarding .45s to the really crazy specimens.

DISTANCE: 75–180 MILES, DEPENDING ON TERRAIN
AND HOW PINK YOU LIKE YOUR LAMB

1 leg of lamb, about 5 pounds, boned and butterflied with
   your bayonet
3 cloves garlic, minced
1 medium onion, minced
$^1/_2$ cup pine nuts, finely chopped
2 teaspoons oregano
Pinch of allspice
Salt and pepper to taste
3 tablespoons full-bodied red wine

At home or on the road, place the lamb, spread out, on foil greased with olive oil. Dust with the garlic, onion, pine nuts, and seasonings, then sprinkle with the red wine. Wrap well, and place on an appropriate engine surface in a big, tough vehicle. Drive until the meat reaches the desired level of doneness. Serve with a packet of MRE rice pilaf, thrown onto the engine for the last 30 minutes.

Veal Rollatini Calabrese alla Passegiata

Several years ago one of us got a dream assignment from *The Washington Post Magazine:* drive the entire coastline of Italy, from France to what was then Yugoslavia. The trip took eighteen days, ran to 2,600 miles, and cost *The Post* only 3,000,000 lire, since we work cheap. Needless to say, Italy being Italy, the best part was pulling into whatever town lay at the end of each day's drive, checking into a nice hotel or a snug little *albergo,* and seeing what was for dinner.

The tenth day of driving found us in Reggio di Calabria, at the tip of the toe of the boot. From Reggio, you can look across the Straits of Messina at Sicily. We arrived at the city just as the early January darkness was falling, and found ourselves trying to inch down the main drag just as everyone in Reggio was turning out for the evening *passegiata.* The *passegiata* is an Italian tradition, especially in the small towns and cities down south. The idea is simple: The citizenry gets dressed up—and in Italy, this doesn't mean putting your baseball cap on forward instead of backward—and strolls along the main street. Not just the sidewalk, the street. It took us forty-five minutes to drive six blocks to our hotel.

After we showered, turned up the lapels on our suit jacket, and put a fresh snap in the brim of the old Borsalino, we sauntered out to join the *passegiata* ourselves. Our path eventually led to a place called Rodrigo's, where we enjoyed a starter of *linguine tramonti rossi,* tossed with cream, caviar, and smoked salmon, followed by *rollatini di Calabria*—veal rolls stuffed with pancetta, mozzarella, and lots of Calabria's signature seasoning, dried hot pepper. About halfway through this wonderful entrée, though, the thought occurred: We could have cooked the veal rolls on the engine of our two-liter Ford Sierra (that year's European Tempo) over the course of the six blocks we covered wedging our way through the *passegiata,* and eaten at the hotel.

We'll stick with Rodrigo's, of course. But keep this in mind if there's a major traffic jam in your future, and a good Italian butcher is nearby.

DISTANCE: 75 MILES OR 6 BLOCKS

$^1/_2$ cup minced pancetta
2 thin veal scallops, lightly pounded
$^1/_2$ cup shredded mozzarella
$^1/_2$ teaspoon red pepper flakes
Salt and pepper to taste

At home, sauté the minced pancetta until translucent. Lightly oil a sheet of foil (olive oil, of course) and place the veal scallops on the foil alongside each other. Sprinkle each scallop with the pancetta, mozzarella, and seasonings. Roll tightly and wrap with the foil to hold the roll shape. Wrap in an additional 2 layers of foil and place on the engine.

NOTE: Wrap the rolls separately if engine space is limited.

East German Car
Cooking: Preunification

When Communist rule collapsed in East Germany, a popular escape vehicle was the Trabant, a sort of Volkswagen of East Germany without the decadent luxury of the Beetle. Thousands of Trabants ran long enough to make it over the nearest border.

In January 1991 John Tagliabue of *The New York Times* described the Trabant as "a cross between a jeep and an amusement park bumper car . . . like a rejection of everything that the German auto industry has learned over the last four decades." With nonrecyclable plastic bodies and rear windows that were glued shut, they were the cars of choice in a society of no choices. Powered by tiny two-cylinder motors, they weren't much for engine cooking, but, with the Communists in power, East Germany wasn't much for food.

We've tried to conjure up what car cooking might have been like when the Wall was a going concern. While some poor housewife has stood in line for hours to buy a few shriveled potatoes and a mushy, frost-struck onion, her husband has lucked out. On the way home from the tractor factory (the bomb factory?), he's managed to swap a pint of supposedly real Russian vodka for 100 grams of fatty pork shin. On their drive to his mother's house in the country, they prepare a hot meal as a surprise.

DRIVING TIME: FOREVER

Stale lard or rancid oil
4 potatoes, peeled and cut into 1/4-inch strips
100 grams pork shin, cut into thin strips

1 small onion, chopped
1 mouthful beer

At home or on the road, smear foil (from the black market) with some lard or oil. Arrange half of the potatoes on the foil. Cover with the pork strips, then sprinkle with the chopped onion. Finish with the remaining potatoes, and moisten all with the beer. If times are flush, add some salt and pepper.

Close the package, then wrap with 2 additional sheets of foil (standard on all our Western recipes, but a real extravagance here). Place on an appropriate part of the Trabi's engine, and hope the car makes it to *Mutter's*.

(Also hope that nothing goes amiss and that the car doesn't catch fire, since the Duroplast body parts, when burned, give off dioxin.)

East German Car Cooking: Postreunification

Back in May of 1989, before Eastern Europe had its lights turned on, we spent a month in Poland (it was cheap, and we were curious). Access from the west was a train trip along the Berlin Corridor, where we were fined ten East German marks for tossing a cigarette butt out the train window; after a night in West Berlin, we checked out the side of the Wall without bullet holes, then walked across the border to get the train to Warsaw.

The few hours in East Berlin before the train left were eye-openers. We had always imagined seeing artillery pockmarks from WW II, and here they were. Inveterate jaywalkers, we waited carefully until the citizenry had started to cross. Happy eaters, we looked at the plates in the cafés and had beers instead. Dog lovers, we watched in the station as guards sent their dogs the length of the train carriages looking for literal hangers-on. Habitually nosy as the day is long, we stopped asking questions. It was the most depressing place we've ever been, including the nether parts of our home states of Rhode Island and New Jersey.

And suddenly (in the long view), it all changed. The Wall came down, and clothing that came in colors other than gray appeared in the East. People started smiling. Complexions improved. With Western capitalism—at least for those who could figure out its rules—came Western accessories, including cars. BMWs and Mercedes in all shades of the rainbow cruised the streets of the old Eastern cities; sleek Porsches were dodging the soon-to-be-filled potholes. It was a brand-new world, with brand-new food.

Imagine, if you will, Helmut and Mathilde, a young couple from Leipzig, taking a weekend jaunt in their Mercedes (unless they decide to take the Porsche 928, a great cooking car). On the trip to the butcher, Helmut, a venture capitalist, takes the wheel as Mathilde, a lawyer, takes a few calls on her cell phone. Before setting off, they also drop in at the wine merchant and the teeming produce market. It will be a lunch touched by the glow of democracy.

DISTANCE: 150 MILES

1 Vidalia onion, imported from Georgia (the American one), thinly sliced

500 grams potatoes, preferably fingerlings or Yukon Gold, coarsely chopped

100 grams *Bindnerfleisch* (air-dried beef from Switzerland), finely chopped

White wine, preferably a Mosel Spatlëse or, in the spirit of the European Union, a first-growth Sauternes

500 grams fresh Strasbourg goose liver, very thinly sliced

Sea salt and freshly ground black pepper

A couple of sprigs of fresh rosemary, plucked from the patio herb garden

At home or on the road, heavily smear a sheet of foil with butter. Arrange half the onion to suit the cooking surface of either the Benz or the 928.

Mix the chopped potatoes with the chopped *Bindnerfleisch* and spread half over the onion. Sprinkle with some wine.

Cover with the liver slices, dust with salt and pepper, and top with the rosemary. Sprinkle again with wine.

Finish with another layer of the potato-*Bindnerfleisch* mixture and the remaining onion. Sprinkle with wine.

Seal the packet, and give it the final 2 wraps. Place on the engine and cook, turning once, until the onion and potatoes are crisped and the liver is about to melt.

Helmut and Mathilde might finish the bottle of white with their lunch, although a good Burgundy—say, a Romanee-Conti—would also be pleasant. Isn't freedom grand?

Toad in the Hole under the Bonnet

One of us—if we may for the moment depart from the editorial "we" that makes us seem like Siamese twins—is an unabashed Anglophile, who drives his family nuts by playing Sir Edward Elgar's *Coronation Ode* at full volume during breakfast, and the other is actually part English. Both of us, however, can fully appreciate the nearly universal disdain that has been heaped upon English food. We've had enough cellophane-wrapped Scotch eggs in pubs, enough overcooked vegetables and mealy gray bangers, to know that the rest of the world didn't make this stereotype up. Worst of all, one of us actually traveled through France—through *France,* for God's sake—with an English couple who packed along their own supply of axle-grease English margarine, lest they should have to eat some of the local butter. We're fully aware that as Americans, we live in a culinary glass house: Some of the world's worst food is served up right here at home. But it generally lacks the special awfulness of the Naugahyde-green mashed peas you get with an order of fish and chips back in Blighty.

And yet . . . and yet (strains of the *Coronation Ode* come up in the background) . . . the English larder, and the traditional English kitchen repertoire, have all the ingredients of a noble cuisine. Think of great joints of beef, rabbit pie, Devonshire clotted cream, steak and kidney pie, poached salmon, and well-hung grouse (no, not that kind of hung—go look up a game cookbook). Think of all the sweet and savory puddings, with the noble plum pudding at the head of the lot (take it, Elgar). English cuisine at its best is the provender for a *Wind in the Willows* idyll, a cold, crisp night in Tolkien's shire, a calm-seas cruise with Aubrey and Maturin and a first-rate cook in the galley.

Then, of course, there are English cars. Traditionally reviled for their mechanical idiosyncracies, their ranks of marques decimated and taken over until even Rolls-Royce seems likely to come under German ownership (fight them on the beaches, perhaps, but not in the boardrooms), English automobiles nevertheless have a cachet that sets them apart from mere functional iron. If the first really fine day of spring doesn't make you want to hop into a Morgan and take off across the downs and dales, you're as hopeless as a poorly hung grouse.

This is a recipe that calls for a deft touch, a little ingenuity, and proper care—rather like owning an old English car. We depart here from our otherwise ironclad caveat regarding loose, gooey stuff, but if you fashion a serviceable foil packet and have the right engine surface available, you should be able to pull this off—or see it through, as the English say.

DISTANCE: 60–75 MILES

1 egg
^{1}/4 teaspoon salt
Pepper to taste
1 cup flour
1 cup milk
^{1}/2 pound small pork sausages—breakfast sausages work
    nicely

At home, before assembling the ingredients, find a secure spot on a hot, flat part of the engine that will accommodate a sturdy foil packet, gently molded as necessary to the surrounding parts. It's a good idea to do a dry run with an empty packet, so you know what you're getting into. To make the packet, start with 3 sheets of regular or 2 sheets of heavy-duty foil, placed atop each other. Bring the sides up and fold/seal the sides to make a little box or tray big enough to hold the batter, remembering that the batter will expand while cooking. Have ready another layer of foil sheets with which to make a lid.

Beat the egg with the salt and pepper, then slowly beat in the flour. Add the milk in a thin stream and beat the batter until creamy. Chill the batter 1 hour.

Poke the sausages with the tines of a sharp fork and fry until lightly browned. Remove from the pan and arrange on the bottom of your foil packet, adding a tablespoon or so of the fat in the pan. Pour the batter over the sausages and crimp the lid onto the packet. Be careful when transporting to the car—you may want to fit the packet in first, then add the ingredients and crimp on the lid.

Drive through the countryside at a stately pace, popping open the bonnet (and the foil lid) from time to time until poking with a toothpick (*not* all the way through to the bottom of the packet!) indicates that the time has come, Ratty and Mole, for your little picnic on the stream bank.

Newfie Cod

In every country, there's a state or province they tell jokes about. In Italy, the people up north make fun of the Calabrians. In Germany, the Frisians are held up as risible clodhoppers. Americans have their rednecks, on whom the South no longer has a monopoly. And the Canadians love to make fun of Newfoundlanders.

Now, the people in Canada's easternmost province aren't all clueless hicks. From what we've seen of them, they're resourceful, hardworking, good-hearted folks with all the economic cards stacked against them—especially since the cod supplies have dried up, and we don't mean into *baccala*. But Newfoundland is Canada's newest province, and the new kid gets the business.

All this is by way of introducing our Newfie recipe with a Newfie joke—one that, of course, involves a car.

Seems a Newfie takes his girl out for a drive, and they end up parked at the end of a dock watching a big moon come up over Bonavista Bay. The guy puts his hand on the girl's knee and leaves it there for a long time.

"You know," she says, "you could go further." So the Newfie puts the car in gear, and drives off the end of the dock.

DISTANCE: 75 MILES (OR ALL THE WAY TO ONTARIO, TO LOOK FOR WORK)

1 cod fillet, about 1 1/2 inches thick
1/2 small onion, sliced and separated into rings
2 tablespoons light cream
2 slices meaty bacon

At home or on the road, butter a sheet of foil well. Place the cod on the foil, and cover with the onion rings. Moisten with the cream, then lay the bacon strips over all. Wrap and place bacon side up on a hot part of the engine; turn when halfway done so the bacon side is down. The fish is done when firm and the bacon is crisp. (If the bacon doesn't get that crisp and you don't like soft bacon, discard it and eat the fish—you've got the bacon flavor.)

PARTING THOUGHTS

When we signed off last time, we posed a whole raft of questions: Should you cook a rump roast on a rear-engine car? How best to do brown rice on the wheezy little four-banger in the back end of a '67 VW bus? Is the Suzuki Samurai the ideal car for baking turnovers? But now that we're staring the big two-oh-oh-oh in the eye, these seem like quaint concerns. Now the overriding question has to do with the future of internal combustion and the technologies that might replace it. If cars go electric, will changing our cooking techniques be as simple as going from gas to electric-range burners? Probably not—cooking in an electric vehicle won't be a matter of using secondhand heat but of tapping into the power supply with specially designed equipment. But will it be worth it? Will it cut thirty-five miles off your cruising range if you plug a waffle iron into your electric car motor? No

small matter, if it takes seventeen hours to charge the batteries. And can you cook on the power plant in a hydrogen-powered vehicle, like the one Daimler-Benz is developing? (We have a "Veal Hindenburg" recipe up our sleeves, just in case.) And there's always the specter of expanded mass transit: How can the government be sure everybody wants to eat the same thing?

So little time, so much to think about. That's why you'll still be able to find us in our old think tank, Schwartz's, on Boulevard St.-Laurent in Montreal.

APPENDIX

RECIPE LIST BY REGION

	WHERE TO DO PREP WORK	APPROXIMATE DISTANCE/MILES
THE NORTHEAST		
Cutlass Cod Supreme (two versions)	Home/Road	40–70
Hyundai Halibut with Fennel	Home/Road	55–85
Merritt Parkway Veal Scallopini	Home/Road	35–40
Veal Chop Forestiere	Home	75
Enzo's Veal	Home/Road	75
Eggs in Purgatory	Home/Road	55
Eggs-On Cheese Pie	Home/Road	55
Pat's Provolone Porsche Potatoes	Home	55
Speedy Spedini	Home	40

	WHERE TO DO PREP WORK	APPROXIMATE DISTANCE/MILES
Down-the-Shore Cavatelli, Sausage, and Broccoli Rabe	Home	70
Thruway Thighs	Home	50–200
Upper-Class Roadkill	Home	70
Stuffed Whole Fish	Home	140
Safe-at-Any-Speed Stuffed Eggplant	Home	165–220

THE MIDWEST

Mom's Tuna Wiggle	Home/Road	55–1,000
Dwight David Eisenhower Pepper Steak	Home/Road	55
Hot Dog Surprise	Home/Road	40
JB's Mall Pups	Home/Road	25–30
Milwaukee Tube Steaks	Home/Road	55–85
Out-of-the-Fire, onto-the-Engine Stew	Home/Road	85
Candy-Apple-Red Chicken	Home	85–110
Cruise-Control Pork Tenderloin	Home/Road	250
Fupped Duck Catera	Home	75
Any-City Chicken Wings	Home	140–200
Lead-Foot Stuffed Cabbage	Home	55
To Grandmother's House Road Turkey	Home	220
Curmudgeon's Capered Lamb	Home/Road	55

	WHERE TO DO PREP WORK	APPROXIMATE DISTANCE/MILES
THE SOUTH		
Good and Simple Cajun Shrimp/Crayfish	Home/Road	35
"Cajun" Shrimp	Home/Road	55
Blackened Roadfish	Home/Road	50
Orange Roughy Floribbean	Home	40
New Orleans Doves	Home	40
U.S. 17 Carolina Stuffed Crabs	Home	40–55
Pickup Ham Steak	Home	85
Maryland Crab Imperial	Home/Road	50
CALIFORNIA AND POINTS WEST		
Poached Fish Pontiac	Home/Road	40
Three-Pepper Salmon Steaks	Home/Road	55
Open Sesame Fillet	Home	50
Abalone Allanté	Home/Road	25–30
Baked Gilroy Garlic Highway 101	Home	55
Melrose Avenue Chicken	Home	55
Donner Pass Red-Flannel Hash	Home/Road	?
Corvette Stingray	Home	55–85
Chicken Breast Lido	Home	140
It's a Wrap	Home/Road	50
INTERNATIONAL		
Nifty NAFTA Nachos	Home/Road	60
Bento Boxster	—	Negligible
MRE Leg of Lamb	Home/Road	75–180

	WHERE TO DO PREP WORK	APPROXIMATE DISTANCE/MILES
Veal Rollatini Calabrese alla Passegiata	Home	75
East German Car Cooking: Preunification	Bleak Apartment Block/Road	Forever
East German Car Cooking: Postunification	Home/Road	150
Toad in the Hole under the Bonnet	Home	60–75
Newfie Cod	Home/Road	75

CHRIS MAYNARD is a professional photographer and the cofounder of the YO-YO School of Art. He lives in Yonkers, New York.

BILL SCHELLER is the author of twenty books and serves as a contributing editor for *National Geographic Traveler* and *Islands* magazines. He lives with his wife and son in Vermont.